Pinter in the Theatre

Ian Smith was born in Wolverhampton in 1963 and lives in London, where he works as a critic, writer and musician. He has held posts as a lecturer in modern and Renaissance literature at the Universities of Oxford, London, Warwick and Boston, and his publications include reviews of theatre, film and music for the *Times Literary Supplement*, the *New Statesman* and BBC Radio 3 and Radio 4, as well as a major forthcoming study of T.S. Eliot.

Ian Smith has worked extensively in theatre, television and radio, as a musician and as an actor of tiny roles. He collaborated with Steve Waters to produce original music for Waters' autobiographical radio work *My Secret Life*, and his settings of four poems by Philip Larkin were broadcast in November 2004 by BBC Radio 3.

Ian Smith and Harold Pinter met in 1988, and have met regularly ever since, discussing cricket, life, and the poems, plays and screenplays of Pinter.

Pinter in the Theatre

Compiled and introduced by
Ian Smith

Foreword by
Harold Pinter

NICK HERN BOOKS
London
www.nickhernbooks.co.uk

A Nick Hern Book

Pinter in the Theatre first published in Great Britain in 2005
by Nick Hern Books Limited, 14 Larden Road, London W3 7ST

Copyright in the compilation, Introduction and interviews
(except as below) © 2005 Ian Smith

Copyright in the reprinted interviews in 'Pinter on Pinter' and
the interview with Peter Hall is vested in the respective sources:
see Acknowledgements

Mick Goldstein's letter to Michael Billington copyright © 1984
Mick Goldstein

Henry Woolf's article copyright © 2002 Henry Woolf,
courtesy of *The Guardian*

Foreword copyright © 2005 Harold Pinter. Printed by permission.
All rights reserved. Applications for any use whatsoever must be made
in advance to Judy Daish Associates Limited, 2 St Charles Place,
London W10 6EG

Ian Smith has asserted his moral right to be identified
as the author of this work

Typeset by Country Setting, Kingsdown, Kent CT14 8ES
Printed and bound in Great Britain by Biddles, King's Lynn

A CIP catalogue record for this book is available from
the British Library

ISBN 1 85459 836 8 (hardback)
ISBN 1 85459 864 3 (paperback)

Contents

Foreword

Ian Smith plays cricket for Gaieties CC. He makes big 100s and his batting average last season was 71. I therefore had every confidence in him when it was proposed that he edit this book. His chosen team certainly play shots all round the wicket.

I've worked in the theatre for over fifty years – as writer, director and actor. (I even designed a play of mine once – *Ashes to Ashes* in Italian in Palermo. I called the designer Gomez.) Actors and directors have therefore been a constant factor in my life. A number of them are dead and some are on the wagon but the ones in this book are certainly alive and kicking. It was a great pleasure for me to work with all of them.

I would not exactly describe any of them as shy, but I have never heard them speak so openly and fully as they do here. I've probably learnt a great deal from their candid and fearless accounts.

HAROLD PINTER

Introduction

First, a few words from Pinter himself:

He is his own man. He's gone his own way from the word go. He follows his nose. It's a pretty sharp one. Nobody pushes him around. He writes what he likes – not what others might like him to write.

But in doing so he has succeeded in writing serious plays which are also immensely popular. You can count on the fingers of one hand those who have brought that off. But, indisputably, he's one of them. He doesn't look fifty either.[1]

This was written by Pinter for the fiftieth birthday of his friend Tom Stoppard, but all of it, with the possible exception of the last sentence, applies equally well to Pinter himself.

Through interviews with Pinter and important collaborators, this book expands on some of Pinter's remarks. It examines how he has 'gone his own way from the word go'. It examines the 'serious' nature of his work, and how it is embedded in the intellectual and political context in which he has spent his life. And it considers something that is occasionally taken for granted in Pinter criticism; that Pinter's work, for audiences wherever it has been played, has always been 'immensely popular'.

All the new interviews for this book focus on the process of making Pinter's plays work in performance, as compelling depictions of human action. In a Pinter drama, an action or motive may on occasion be unexpected or even inexplicable, but the mystery is intriguing only to the extent that the character or the relationship involved is credible and interesting. This living theatrical life of the characters, and through them of the plays, is a prerequisite for the intellectual depth of the plays, not an addition or complement to it. As Pinter has said, if a living performance does not take place, intellectual resonance 'cannot exist'.

This introduction deals mainly with Pinter's background, education, and early years in the theatre. A detailed account of his entire career, or of critical debates around his work, would be impossible in the space available, and in any case the formative years are of special importance for any writer. This focus is especially justified here because of Pinter's remarkable emergence, around his thirtieth birthday, with a striking, innovative and entirely coherent style that offered distinctive challenges, as well as great rewards, to players and audiences. That style has seen many developments and experiments over more than forty years. But definitive artistic and intellectual elements of Pinter's work have been present from the start. In this book, the introduction examines the origins of this style, and the actors and directors describe how it is put into practice. The interviews offer comment on Pinter's training in the theatre, and on the mechanics of rehearsing and performing his work.

Two very significant critical points emerge from the study of Pinter's background and intellectual development: first, that his writing and thought have always been inseparable from political concerns that were omnipresent in his early life; second, that from a precociously early age Pinter has been a committed and self-conscious intellectual – not merely a person of what the British call 'highbrow' taste, but one who scrutinises and mediates his experience through a body of knowledge and a critical apparatus acquired and developed through learning and debate. To argue, as some do, that in his intellectualism Pinter is not being 'true to his roots' is to reveal ignorance both of him and of the rich cultural life of the communities in which he grew up and then studied and worked in his early years (if anything, it is in the more privileged and wealthy circles in which he now sometimes moves that Pinter's intellectualism and seriousness appear most often to create unease).

Pinter's achievement is the product of a complex individual sensibility and immense talent, but also of his background and early years: the family circumstances, the intellectual and political influences, and a decade of furious work in the theatre, which combined to form him as a writer.

★

Tell me more, with all the authority and brilliance you can muster, about the socio-politico-economic structure of the environment in which you attained to the age of reason.

Spooner to Hirst in No Man's Land, *Act I*

Pinter was born on 10 October 1930, in Hackney, East London. His father and mother were children of Jewish immigrants whose families hailed from Central or Eastern Europe. Three of his grandparents were from Odessa. His father, Jack, worked as a jobbing tailor and as a 'cutter': in bespoke tailoring it is the cutter, not the proprietor of a shop who is the better craftsman, shaping cloth to create style and flatter individual physiques. According to one actor who met him, Jack Pinter was also a champion Charleston dancer in the 1920s (Pinter has told me that in the early 1960s he enjoyed dancing to jazz). Pinter's mother and other members of the family were interested in the arts, especially music.

He did not have a religious upbringing, and, though issues of the human spirit and the 'uncanny' have intrigued him in recent years, he says that the last religious ceremony he attended, apart from weddings and funerals, was his bar mitzvah at the age of thirteen. Nevertheless, Pinter believes that Jewishness has been significant in shaping his personality and his writing. More than perhaps any other prominent British writer of his time, he has drawn on and developed twentieth-century aesthetic traditions that were forged in Europe in conditions of upheaval, deracination and alienation of many kinds. It has often been noted that most of the literary canon of Modernism was written by exiles and emigrés, many of whom were working in a language or idiom that was not their first, subjecting even the most commonplace words and phrases to an intense and productive scrutiny. Pinter's Jewish-immigrant background placed him squarely in this tradition. None of his four grandparents spoke English as a first language.

The claustrophobic and intense domestic relations of many of the plays seem to Pinter's old friends, among others, another part of his 'Yiddishkeit' (the term used in conversation with me by his lifelong friend Henry Woolf). Warren Mitchell, an actor of similar age and background to Pinter, grew convinced while rehearsing the role of Max in *The Homecoming*, that the character should be played as a Jewish patriarch, though he said that when he put this to Pinter, he was only met with a 'seraphic smile'.[2] Religious faith and textual exegesis have a closer and more explicit relationship in Judaism than in many Christian traditions, and certainly the power and seriousness of literature was recognised in the Jewish culture that Pinter inhabited (Susan Engel emphasises this in her interview). In his autobiographical speech on accepting the David Cohen Prize in 1995, Pinter recalls that 'There was no money to buy books', and that when he did manage to save up the money to buy James Joyce's *Ulysses*, his father refused to allow it on the shelf in the room where his mother served dinner.[3] In the memories of Pinter and his friends, Jewishness reinforced the twin senses of vocation and alienation in young men striving to embark on artistic and intellectual careers from a working-class culture in which books were an expensive, and perhaps even subversive, luxury.

Another feature of the Hackney Jewish community that echoes in the plays is the frequency with which names were changed. In the 1980s an old school contemporary saw Pinter on television and wrote to him giving brief details of what had happened to a number of classmates. Several had changed their names – names that in the first place had only been Anglicisations. A long-standing verbal trick, used by anti-Semites and others, is to create mock-Jewish names like 'Krapstein', and in letters and conversation, Pinter's friends would make this device their own, addressing Mick Goldstein, for example, as 'Weinblatt' or such, with no explanation offered or needed.

In many of Pinter's plays the names of characters are uncertain, debated, or changed with no apparent reason. Pinter has said that when writing he names characters only by letters (A, B, C, D, etc), and experimented with the spelling 'Pinta' when his first published poems appeared in 1950 (in *Poetry London*, a small, influential and notoriously eccentric literary magazine). Pinter was justifiably offended when an academic wrote to him in the 1980s asking why he had chosen to 'repress' his Jewishness in young adulthood by taking the stage name David Baron. Pinter felt not only that it was a perfectly natural thing for an actor to do, but that the name he chose was if anything more Jewish than the one on his birth certificate (Baron was his grandmother's maiden name, though he had apparently forgotten this when he chose it).

During the Second World War, Pinter, like thousands of children, was evacuated from London to escape the Blitz. He went to Cornwall. In addition to the obvious disturbances of being abruptly separated from home and family, evacuation introduced Pinter and his friends to parts of Britain and British culture where they were considered neither normal nor, at times, especially welcome. The broader experience of wartime adolescence left him and his friends with convictions which they say have remained fundamental: of the precariousness of life and the centrality to it of art and culture, of the importance of sexuality and friendship, and of the dangerous corruptibility of states, politicians and officials.

In 1944 Pinter passed the required examination to attend Hackney Downs School. This was one of the state grammar schools, offering free of charge the kind of intense education to the age of eighteen that had hitherto been available only privately. At Hackney Downs, Pinter was to develop many lifelong interests. After literature, his main love was cricket, a game he would play at a good amateur standard into his sixties. He has written prose and poetry about the game, and there are references to cricket and cricketers in many of his plays. His most exceptional sporting talent, however, was sprinting, and he broke the school records for 100 and 200 yards (temporarily losing the friendship of one opponent, the future head of a Cambridge college).

Friends regarded Pinter's athletic success with a mixture of admiration and disgust, since he achieved it while indulging precociously in the supposedly crippling delights of smoking and going out with girls. He has retained a typical sprinter's build, which is a part of his formidable stage (and offstage) presence: he is just under six feet tall, strongly built with powerful legs and shoulders, and with a deep chest housing the big lungs needed for explosive action.

In his Cohen Prize speech Pinter records a crucial relationship begun at Hackney Downs:

In 1944 I met Joseph Brearley, who came to the school to teach English. Brearley was a tall Yorkshireman who suffered from malaria, had been torpedoed at sea during the war and possessed a passionate enthusiasm for English poetry and dramatic literature. There had been no drama in the school when he arrived in 1945 but before we knew where we were he announced that he would do a production of Macbeth *and pointing at me in class said: 'And you, Pinter, will play* Macbeth.' 'Me, sir?' *I said.* 'Yes. You,' *he said. I was fifteen and I did play Macbeth, in modern dress, wearing the uniform of a major-general. My parents gave me the* Collected Plays *of* Shakespeare *to mark the occasion . . .*

Joe Brearley and I became close friends. We embarked on a series of long walks, which continued for years, starting from Hackney Downs, up to Springfield Park, along the River Lea, back up Lea Bridge Road, past Clapton Pond, through Mare Street to Bethnal Green. Shakespeare dominated our lives at that time (I mean the lives of my friends and me) but the revelation which Joe Brearley brought with him was John Webster. On our walks, we would declare into the wind, at the passing trolley-buses or indeed the passers-by, nuggets of Webster, such as:

> *What would it pleasure me to have my throat cut*
> *With diamonds? Or to be smothered*
> *With Cassia? Or to be shot to death with pearls?*
> *I know death hath ten thousand several doors*
> *For men to take their exits: and 'tis found*
> *They go on such strange geometric hinges*
> *You may open them both ways: anyway, for heaven's sake,*
> *So I were out of your whispering.*
>
> The Duchess of Malfi

That language made me dizzy.
Joe Brearley fired my imagination. I can never forget him.[4]

The use of the word 'can' in that last sentence (where 'will' or 'could' would be more usual) is typical of Pinter, combining a fastidious and slightly unorthodox use of language with strong and enduring emotion. The walks and the friendship are commemorated in Pinter's poem 'Joseph Brearley, 1909-77 (Teacher of English)'.

Brearley retained his penchant for declaiming dramatic verse, and years later in New York, shortly before his death, he dismissed a beggar with words from *King Lear*. Those who knew Brearley were sure that he had the imagination and physical presence to have been a successful actor, but his vocation was as a teacher. This vocation had been fired in its turn by F.R. Leavis, and others, in the Cambridge University English school of the interwar years. That school was then one of the most dynamic and influential of all university departments: one which transformed the young subject of English from a marginal academic discipline into one with a unique aura of excitement, contemporaneity and relevance.

For graduates of the Cambridge school such as Brearley, the essential link between serious literature and a healthy society was axiomatic. Many believed that the best literature of their time (and even that of other times, especially the late Tudor and Jacobean period) offered not only the most telling comment on contemporary society but the best means of engaging with it or of altering its state of crisis. For the leader of the Cambridge school, I.A. Richards, literature was a means of 'saving us' from the disasters of the modern world; a world in which the whole apparatus of party politics was seen to be irretrievably discredited.

Though Pinter never went to university, and appears to have spent little of his time at drama schools in formal study, his career remained indebted, through Brearley first of all, to academic English in its early years of heroic optimism. This underpins his enduring certainty of literature's aesthetic value, intellectual seriousness, and historical force. In this way, Pinter's literary thought has always been both intellectual and 'political'. His formative years were enmeshed in the politics of community, religion, class and war. And his intellectual and literary grounding took the political and dissident force of literature not as something that might be argued, but as a fundamental point of departure.

During his teens, Pinter became part of a group of Hackney friends who shared a passionate commitment to literature, discussion, cricket and verbal humour. The group included Henry Woolf (who became a distinguished actor and Professor of Theatre), Mick Goldstein (a violinist and writer), Morris Wernik (a Professor of English in Canada), Jimmy Law (Head of English at Worth School) and Ron Percival. Exceptionally intelligent and intellectually precocious, this group played an important role in stimulating Pinter in his formative years, and if he was ever their leader, it was as the first among equals. Pinter has retained the friendship and loyalty of this group throughout his life. Versions of several of them appear in his writing, especially in the early novel and play *The Dwarfs*. Two have contributed to this volume: Mick Goldstein, to whom Pinter's collection of plays *Other Places* is dedicated, and Henry Woolf, who commissioned, directed and acted in Pinter's first play, *The Room*, and has continued to work with him ever since.

With little or no disposable income, the group spent much of their time walking about London visiting parks and public libraries, and accumulating an eclectic range of interests that included contemporary poetry, philosophy, cricket literature, Hollywood and European film, the London night-bus network, classical music and jazz. Above all, Pinter likes to recall that Shakespeare 'dominated our lives'.

Conversation with Woolf, Goldstein or Pinter himself is an education in an important source of the dramatic Pinteresque. It is a mode of conversing that at first can seem almost anarchic but which over time reveals strict rules. Small talk is absent, and any that is offered will fall on stony ground. Humour is constant, but in the context of an obligatory underlying seriousness. Any personal opinion is admissible, so long as it is stated as only that. Facts must be verified. A careless or pretentious use of language is immediately satirised, often through repetition. Mutual respect is required, but any hint of self-importance is mercilessly ridiculed.

The Hackney group gave Pinter a founding set of intellectual interests and personal relationships of a kind that other writers find at university (though few of them with comparable depth). But the fact that so much of Pinter's intellectual grounding took place outside institutional education was of tremendous importance for his writing. His taste and interests retained the voracious energy and quirkiness of the outsider and autodidact. Had Pinter been more conventionally schooled, it might well have been more difficult for his early writing to rekindle as it did the dynamism and freshness of modernist writing, with its *bricolage*, spontaneity, and oblique new perspectives. Pinter also never learned to be a cultural snob, or that one who enjoyed reading James Joyce should necessarily despise writers of more conventional novels. In the 1960s, Philip Larkin was surprised that Pinter was an enthusiastic (and influential) advocate of his poetry. Since the plays were 'rather modern', he wrote to Pinter, 'I shouldn't have thought my grammar school Betjeman would have appealed to you.' Unlike Pinter, Larkin had been to Oxford, where he learned that the mixing of Modern and Traditional was 'not done'.

In 1948 Pinter took up a state scholarship to the Royal Academy of Dramatic Art. He found the institution intolerable, and to escape classes while retaining his government grant he faked a nervous breakdown towards the end of his first year. He recalls that after leaving his final interview with the head of the Academy, ashen and subdued according to character, he met two friends round the corner. All three immediately sprinted full-tilt for a bus to the cricket at Lord's. As they turned into the ground to see the green turf stretched out in the afternoon sun, Pinter vividly remembers that a late cut sent the ball skimming towards them – 'it was one of the happiest days of my life'. The following months were, he says, a fruitful time spent 'mooching about', reading and writing, though he regretted lying to his parents about the plays he claimed to be acting in at RADA.[5]

In the year he joined RADA, Pinter was called up for National Service. Two years in the armed forces were then compulsory for all fit men aged eighteen. Pinter refused to go. He declared himself a conscientious objector but was not a pacifist, and insists that had he been older during the war against Hitler and Fascism he would certainly have done military service, either as conscript or volunteer. He was summoned to a tribunal where 'I simply said I disapproved of the Cold War and wasn't going to help it along as a boy of eighteen . . . I really did think very clearly about the millions of people who had been killed in the war, the war to end wars, and the tragic farce of starting the Cold War almost before the hot war had finished.' Both the local and the appeal ('Appellate') tribunal found this inadequate as 'Grounds of Conscience', and at the subsequent trials Pinter was twice fined. (His father had to borrow the money to pay the fines.) He knew, especially at the second hearing, that a prison sentence was the more usual sanction for an able-bodied non-pacifist and, as he puts it, 'I took my toothbrush to the trials.'[6]

The Hiroshima and Nagasaki bombs, and the immediate military and diplomatic tensions between the USA and the USSR, meant that Pinter and his friends grew up, they recall, believing that a secular apocalypse was imminent and inevitable. Henry Woolf says: 'We were the first generation, we thought, who will never live to see our children grow up.'[7] If Pinter's characters, especially in early plays, inhabit a world of paranoia, suspicion and terrifying external forces that cannot be fully known, it is neither surprising, nor without 'political' significance. Harold Hobson, in the sole appreciative review of *The Birthday Party* on its first appearance in London, commented in the *Sunday Times* that 'Mr Pinter has got hold of a primary fact of existence. We live on the verge of disaster.'[8]

Woolf also shares Pinter's memory that during the war, 'the sense of the Gestapo was very strong in England. They weren't here, but we as children knew about them.' On a lesser but nonetheless significant scale the Cold War paranoia of Western governments brought suspicion and persecution on their own populations. In the United States, the McCarthy investigations persecuted those who had at any time shown sympathy with left-wing causes, and in Britain there was a similar climate in some quarters, as Mick Goldstein's anecdote below shows. A fear of enemies within and an urge to promote the nation's moral and spiritual health brought a sharp rise in prosecutions for homosexual 'crimes', especially after the exposure of the Soviet spies Burgess and MacLean. Several actors, including John Gielgud, were among those prosecuted and convicted. Gielgud was fined, others sent to prison. This was a part of the context in which Pinter devised the persecution of Aston in *The Caretaker* and Stanley in *The Birthday Party*, and in which *The Hothouse* was conceived.

Meanwhile, in the East End of London, fascism itself remained a real threat. Leaving the Hackney Boys' Club late at night could be hazardous for young Jewish men. Mick Goldstein recalls an incident in Ridley Road, near the junction of Ball's Pond Road:

We had decided to attend a meeting of the British National Party (or whatever they were called at the time) and Jimmy [Law] was carrying a book under his arm (probably a volume of Baudelaire). He was suddenly pointed at and accused of being a Commie, at which he held his book aloft and called out, 'Why – because I can read?' Of course we thought this was very funny. We left the meeting followed by a group carrying things like broken bottles and bicycle chains. [9]

The scene hints at the dramatic Pinteresque: tension and threatened violence are mediated by irony, humour and literary seriousness, underpinned by an unmistakeable readiness to stand and fight if necessary. Challenged by fascists, Pinter and his friends hold up not a broken bottle or bicycle chain but a book – and a complex, intellectual and 'foreign' book at that. Far from being a withdrawal from British politics, Pinter's literary tastes have always had an evident political significance: as Pinter comments in his *Paris Review* interview, evidently drawing on the same experiences as Goldstein, 'they'd interpret your very, very being, especially if you had books under your arm, as evidence of your being a communist.'

Pinter and his friends were contemptuous of fascism but vividly conscious of the dangers it carried. Had they grown up in the 1930s this, and their general sense of political and social malaise, would probably have pushed them to join socialist or Marxist political groups. However, by the early years of the Cold War the crimes of the Soviet Union had drastically undermined the idealistic claims which had been made for state Marxism a generation earlier by young writers like W.H. Auden, George Orwell and many others. Khruschev's speech to the Soviet Communist Party in 1958 denounced Stalin and admitted that millions had been killed by his government's social policies and purges of opponents. In political thought, Soviet communism was no longer seen as the antithesis of fascism but was linked with it as a form of state tyranny, under the new term 'totalitarianism' (introduced to general currency in important works by Hannah Arendt and Franz Borkenau in 1948 and 1949).

So for Pinter and his peers there appeared to be, at least in public life, no single political or philosophical alternative to a capitalist society whose failings had been vividly delineated by many of the great twentieth-century artists whom they so admired. In *The Cocktail Party* (the biggest critical and commercial success of the London and New York stage in 1949-50), T.S. Eliot voiced the prevailing mood of many intellectuals: 'the best of a bad job is all any of us make of it.' Pinter, given his temperament as well as his religious background, was never likely to concur with Eliot's rider, 'except of course the saints'. Unlike W.H. Auden, Graham Greene, Edith Sitwell, William Golding and many other literary celebrities of the 1940s and 1950s, Pinter would not be turning to Christianity in response to a terminally pessimistic assessment of the secular world.

The quick succession of wars hot and cold had instilled an acute sense of history and personal responsibility. The British Labour government of 1945 offered, briefly, an idealistic and dynamic cause to fight for in public politics (Pinter's close friend Barry Foster was emphatic in making this point in his interview). Yet by the 1950s Pinter and his peers were faced by the same apparent intellectual vacuum as Eliot and the older generation.[10] There was no conducive political movement for them to join, and Britain, unlike Germany or France, also lacked any institutional tradition of serious sociology or political philosophy that was easy for them to enter. Mick Goldstein recalls that philosophy was an important subject of discussion among Pinter's friends, but the dominant traditions in English philosophy in the 1950s suggested that philosophy might lead away from, rather than toward, a broad set of ethical convictions or concrete actions. Goldberg in *The Birthday Party* and Lenny and Ruth in *The Homecoming* use philosophical debate, in the very distinctive British style of the 1950s, to effect bullying and obfuscation rather than consensus or enlightenment. Lenny's brother Teddy haughtily comments that the 'references' in his academic writing would be beyond his family's comprehension. Philosophy or philosophical language is used to lay claim to social prestige and interpersonal power, and, if the arguments have a meaning beyond that, it seems to be that the world is much harder to know or engage with than might be thought.

In this intellectual and historical climate, then, the danger was that a young man of progressive convictions might be condemned to operate *in*, but not *on*, the world, as Ron Percival apparently accused Pinter in around 1950. Henry Woolf insists that the most important of all the Shakespearean lines which recurred in his conversations with Pinter was Hamlet's 'I could be bounded in a nutshell and count myself a king of infinite space.' In the absence of an enlightened consensual system of human or political understanding, the most important and inviolable freedom seemed to be the one in one's own head: subjective and intellectual autonomy appearing the one safe haven for enlightened self-government. But the more such freedom is sought, the greater the danger of solipsism, isolation or paranoia, for the self who is entirely self-determining has nothing to act as support when personal confidence fails. Hamlet's qualification, as Woolf and Pinter knew and still know, is 'But that I have bad dreams.'

One solution to the problems of alienation, rage and pessimism was to turn them round and make them not responses to a condition, but a condition or even a set of virtues in themselves. In May 1956 Colin Wilson's *The Outsider* was published to rapturous reviews, and quickly became the most successful philosophical and literary-critical work of the decade in terms of sales, reception and prominence. Wilson's work gathered information about a range of real and fictional characters from literature and philosophy (including Van Gogh, Nietzsche, Blake, heroes from Sartre, Camus, Joyce, Hesse and Dostoevsky) to construct a portrait of the hero of the time: the exile, stranger or marginal figure. This hero insisted on posing questions about the 'problem of *pattern* or *purpose* in life' and was a man who sees 'too deep and too much'. He could not consider his own or anyone else's existence '*necessary*' and was 'cut off from other people by an intelligence that ruthlessly destroys their values'. These characters, Wilson maintained, had always been persecuted but would now occupy their true place at the centre of the cultural stage.

Wilson was from Leicester, born in 1931, and his success was part of the wider media phenomenon of the 'Angry Young Man'. This media term grouped writers who had no shared manifesto, and differed hugely in the solutions they offered, though they were indeed young, male and dissenting.

Even to the limited extent that the Angry Young Men formed a coherent group, Pinter was not one of them. But the Angries form an important part of his context. First, because the work of these writers describes some of the essential political and intellectual conditions in which Pinter's early work was formed (though his artistic response was vastly more original and complex than theirs). Second, because their prominence and success illustrate some of the rapid changes in British arts at the time, and the popularity of the term shows that the social conditions to which it was linked were very much part of the fifties' and early sixties' *zeitgeist*.

These were times when rapid social change was soon to be manifested to an unusual extent in the theatre. In 1961, recalling the commercial failure of the first London production of *The Birthday Party*, Pinter commented: 'Very possibly if *The Caretaker* had been put on two years ago the same thing would have applied. There has been some change of climate that I cannot define; some change in the theatregoing public itself, or an adjustment of the public

[23]

taste to certain developments in the drama.'[11] Pinter insisted in the same interview that he was 'not a sociologist', but he was well aware of the social changes to which the new theatre public was linked. He was himself a grammar-school boy who had won a state scholarship to higher education, and whose work had been supported by the BBC acting in its Reithian mode of patrician liberal pluralism. He knew that the rapid expansion of education that followed the Second World War in Britain, and the founding of state bodies like the Arts Council (originally the Council for the Encouragement of Music and the Arts) had created a new constituency of theatregoers.

There is strong evidence that this educated and upwardly mobile group formed a disproportionately high percentage of the audience for new plays in the sixties. Statistics are available for productions at the National Theatre, the Glasgow Citizens' Theatre, and the West End production of *The Man in the Glass Booth*: a play about the trial of a Nazi for crimes against Jews written by Pinter's friend Robert Shaw and directed by Pinter. Between 55 and 80% of the audience were under 35, 18-35% were students, and a further 23-48% had completed higher education. Thus, at a time when graduates formed 3.7% of the national population they and their successors were filling up to 83 per cent of theatres in London and the provinces. And a high proportion of these young graduates were from the provinces, or 'provincial' universities, or indeed both.[12]

In this context, Pinter's work of the 1960s enjoyed huge commercial success, despite the bemusement of many magazine and newspaper critics, whose taste and expectations had been formed in earlier times, when Pinter's combination of high intellectual intensity and lower-class settings might well have amounted to box-office poison.

In 1951 Pinter studied briefly at the Central School of Speech and Drama. But his most important course of theatrical education may be said to have begun in September that year, when he joined the Anew McMaster Company, touring in Ireland with eleven plays, seven of them by Shakespeare. McMaster was the last of the great actor-managers, directing and starring in classic plays performed to big, popular audiences in a tradition that stretched back over a century. Pinter's essay 'Mac' commemorates the time he spent in the company. It is one of his most important pieces of autobiographical writing: a vivid testament to his love of the theatre and to his detailed insight into the power and craft of McMaster's acting.[13]

Soon after joining the company, Pinter recommended his friend Barry Foster to McMaster, and Foster's interview for this volume adds some details to Pinter's account of work with the company. Foster emphasises that, though Pinter makes no mention of this in his essay, McMaster was immensely impressed by Pinter's intelligence, energy, 'scholarship', and great gifts as a Shakespearean actor. According to Foster, McMaster even saw Pinter as his 'successor'. Pinter notes in his essay that McMaster's influence in the major centres of the English theatre was extremely limited. Had it been greater, the balance between acting and writing in Pinter's career may have been very different.

In 1953 Pinter worked in London with another great leading actor of the old school, Donald Wolfit. Wolfit had been one of his boyhood heroes, the star of the first play he went to see, *King Lear* (see the interview for *The Paris Review*). To this day, Pinter can recall and impersonate, with relish and professional admiration, nuances of Wolfit's style. From 1954-59 Pinter acted and toured in repertory companies in places such as Whitby, Birmingham, Eastbourne, Huddersfield, Colchester, Worthing, Palmers Green and many more. He recalls that 'my forte was sinister parts.' Almost all the interviewees for this volume are convinced that this work was essential to Pinter's sense of stagecraft, and to his great responsiveness, as writer and director, to the needs and problems of actors. As one of them put it, 'unlike a lot of writers and directors he knows what it's like to be in the rep trenches – to have to go over the top on a wet matinee afternoon in Frinton when you've been up half the night trying to learn your lines.'[14]

This was by no means avant-garde work. It was the conventional mix of the commercial theatre at the time, with a high proportion of comedies and thrillers. Only belatedly has Pinter's debt to this work been acknowledged by critics. For many years he was seen exclusively as an innovative genius descended from continental and avant-garde dramatists (some of whom he had, in fact, never come across). But it is now argued, by critics and by actors such as Douglas Hodge (in his interview for this book), that in dialogue as well as structure Pinter has affinities with earlier writers like Coward, Rattigan and Wilde, despite the very different settings and tone of their plays. As late as 2000 one reviewer of *The Room* referred to Noël Coward having been deeply 'bored' by the play, without apparently knowing that Coward was one of Pinter's warmest early admirers. 'The Master', along with Richard Burton, Elizabeth Taylor and others, gave private money to finance the film version of *The Caretaker*. He also wrote to Pinter at length praising *The Homecoming*, and including the comment: 'You cheerfully break every rule of writing for the theatre except the cardinal one of never boring for a split-second.'

However, throughout his years as a jobbing actor, Pinter was also steeping himself in a very different literary and theatrical influence. While touring in Ireland with McMaster, he first encountered the work of Samuel Beckett, the most important and direct of the influences on his dramatic writing.

In I think 1951, having read an extract from Beckett's Watt *in a magazine called* Irish Writing, *I looked for books by Beckett in library after library – with no success. Eventually I unearthed one – his first novel,* Murphy. *It had been hanging about Bermondsey Public Reserve Library since 1938. I concluded that interest in Beckett was low and decided to keep it – on an extended loan, as it were. I still have it.*[15]

It would be difficult to overstate Pinter's admiration for Beckett, the friend and true heir of James Joyce, or the extent to which he has found his writing an inspiration. Beckett was also to give indirect aid to Pinter's career, since the great success of *Waiting for Godot* in 1957 demonstrated that innovative drama could have commercial success on the London stage. After writing *The Caretaker*, Pinter sent a copy to Beckett, initiating a deep and loving friendship which lasted until Beckett's death in 1985.

In 1956 Pinter married the actress Vivien Merchant, and in 1958 their son Daniel was born. A woman of striking beauty and presence, Vivien Merchant initially enjoyed greater success on the stage than her husband, and she took the leading female parts in the first productions of several Pinter plays, including *The Homecoming, The Lover* and *Old Times*. In theatrical terminology, as the first to take these parts, she 'created' them, and there is no doubt in the minds of many colleagues that the term was especially appropriate in these cases. Though Pinter insists in his interview for *The Paris Review* that the parts were not written specifically for his wife ('I just think she's a very good actress'), Vivien Merchant's powerful personality and great professional gifts contributed significantly to many of Pinter's major female characters.

The marriage also endured difficulties. Throughout his life Pinter has been an incurable, and occasionally impulsive, romantic, and it is well known that the play *Betrayal* draws heavily on his relationship with the television presenter and critic Joan Bakewell. The growth of Pinter's international reputation and commitments coincided with an inevitable transition in Vivien Merchant's career, away from younger parts and romantic leads and into character and supporting roles. Where *The Lover* and *The Homecoming* drew on Merchant's personal and theatrical verve to portray relationships of intense sexuality and feeling, the work of the later 1960s and early 1970s, particularly *Old Times*, present characters for whom such emotions are coming to be seen in retrospect. By the early 1970s the Pinters' marriage appears to have broken down.

In 1957, the year after his marriage, Pinter wrote his first play, *The Room*, to be performed at the Bristol University

Drama Department, starring and directed by his old friend Henry Woolf, a graduate student there. Woolf is a man of considerable *chutzpah* as well as genuine intellectual and theatrical rigour. Pinter at that time was writing a good deal of poetry, but Woolf forced him to write a play (something he had never done before) by explaining that the theatre was already booked, having first booked the theatre by saying to the university that the 'excellent' play was already written. It was after this production that Pinter was introduced by Susan Engel to Jimmy Wax, who became his literary agent and, in Pinter's phrase, 'my backbone'.[16] Engel, in her interview for this book, recalls the experience of acting in this first production. She insists that though the play puzzled the older academics at Bristol, it struck a chord immediately both with the actors and with the students in the audience.

It is worth pausing over the way various contributors to this book give details of the genesis of *The Room*. Pinter recalls looking through a door by chance and seeing a scene that was the germ of the play: 'a little man cutting bread and making bacon and eggs for a very big man.' Douglas Hodge mentions that of the two men in the scene one was the well-known writer and personality Quentin Crisp. Pinter has had innumerable opportunities in interviews to put these elements together into a classic and irresistible theatrical anecdote, combining celebrities, a bohemian setting, a chance event, Crisp's unconventional sexual and domestic arrangements, and so on. When he chooses to be, Pinter is a masterful raconteur. But, unlike many writers, he is extremely sparing in the use of this gift to describe, contextualise or explain his own work. He prefers to let the characters (and the actors) speak for themselves.

Inspired by the success of *The Room* with university audiences, Pinter wrote *The Birthday Party* largely while acting in rep. The celebrated interrogation scene was composed in a dressing-room during a run of *Doctor in the House*. In April to May 1958 *The Birthday Party* made a successful short tour, being well reviewed and received in Oxford, Cambridge and Wolverhampton. In May, Pinter recalls, it opened in London:

The Birthday Party *opened at the Lyric, Hammersmith, was massacred by the critics (with the exception of Harold Hobson), and was taken off after eight performances. I decided to pop in to the Thursday matinee. I was a few minutes late and the curtain had gone up. I ran up the stairs to the dress circle. An usherette stopped me. 'Where are you going?' she said. 'To the dress circle,' I said, 'I'm the author.' Her eyes, as I recall, misted over. 'Oh are you?' she said, 'Oh, you poor chap. Listen, the dress circle's closed, but why don't you go in, go in and sit down, darling, if you like, go on.' I went into the empty dress circle and looked down into the stalls. Six people were watching the performance, which, I must say, didn't seem to be generating much electricity. I still have the box-office returns for the week. The Thursday matinee brought in two pounds six shillings.*[17]

Harold Hobson's review appeared in the *Sunday Times* on 25 May, the day after the play closed. Hobson, the leading newspaper critic of the time, wrote that he was 'willing to risk whatever reputation I have as a judge of plays by saying that *The Birthday Party* is not a Fourth, not even a Second, but a First; and that Mr Pinter, on the evidence of this work, possesses the most original, disturbing, and arresting talent in theatrical London.'

Though too late to save the production, the review was invaluable to Pinter and to Jimmy Wax. It would be wrong, however, to suggest that Pinter's career was rescued by one good notice. The failure of the Hammersmith production of *The Birthday Party* was not the start of Pinter's dramatic career. It was a violent but brief disruption in a career already established on solid foundations after a decade of acting, several publications in small but respected magazines, and two plays (*The Room* and the touring *Birthday Party*) that had been successful with audiences and critics.

In his *Paris Review* interview, Pinter describes how he persevered with writing in 1958 and 1959, helped by encouragement from his wife and a commission from the BBC resulting in *A Slight Ache*.

In 1960 Pinter's career as a major dramatist in the public eye was inaugurated by the commercial and critical triumph of the first London production of *The Caretaker*. This began a run of remarkable success during the 1960s, which included the revival of *The Birthday Party* and, in 1965, *The Homecoming*, which Pinter has often said he regards as his best work, and was then his first play for five years. He also wrote a number of shorter plays and television plays, and began a series of major screenplays – five major films from Pinter scripts were released between 1963 and 1971. Pinter's screenplays are all adaptations of novels by other writers, and he is conscientious in remaining true to the original author, but their style, and the changes made to plot and character, are unmistakably Pinter's own. (Most of the screen time of *The Servant* is occupied with entirely fresh material extrapolated by Pinter from Robin Maugham's flimsy novella, and *The French Lieutenant's Woman* sets a complete modern plot in parallel with John Fowles' Victorian characters.)

The triumphant success of Pinter's plays, especially with committed theatregoers and with younger audiences, was balanced by a certain amount of unease in some other quarters: several television productions, broadcast in prime time to a public with three channels to choose from, boosted Pinter's remarkable prominence in general British culture. The plays were at times enigmatic and required a high level of close attention. They dealt with 'difficult' subject matter, especially psychological and sexual problems and conflicts, and they portrayed complicated and at times unpleasant personalities. They were also difficult to categorise generically (one reason, perhaps, why the 'Pinter play' became so quickly recognised as a genre in its own right). There was doubt, all in all, over what precisely audiences were taking such pleasure in witnessing: in August 1960 Pinter contributed to a discussion in the *Sunday Times* over whether it was appropriate that audiences for *The Caretaker* should be laughing so very much at a play involving so much sadness and suffering. These questions of genre and tone have remained problematic for some of the plays' audiences, critics and performers. They are at the heart of all the interviews with actors and directors for this book.

One further aspect of the plays has remained at the heart of discussion and treatments of Pinter, even though it is rarely stated explicitly. Pinter's dramatic work of the 1960s achieved something that had hitherto seemed impossible, by using much of the intellectual and stylistic inheritance of Modernism in plays that were nevertheless well-structured, dramatically satisfying and commercially successful. In form as well as in content, the exhilarating contemporaneity and intellectualism of Pinter's work departed abruptly from the prevailing conventions of the West End, but somehow escaped what had been seen as modernist drama's inevitable vices of the fragmentary, the impersonal and the didactic. This caused confusion not only for opponents of 'modern drama' but also for some advocates who might have assumed that a truly contemporary dramatist would have little time for such old-fashioned notions as character, emotion or plot. This question also is implicitly discussed by all the actors who discuss the demands of playing Pinter, and in particular the need to balance a respect for the studied and formal elements of the writing with a commitment to credible and dynamic characters.

The interviews from this period illustrate a range of critical perspectives and responses to the work, and are included for what they say about the climate of response as well as for what they say about Pinter. Pinter's own responses in interview demonstrate an approach to 'explaining' the plays that he has retained throughout his career. He insists that he finds his material in life around him; that his characters are real, and the comedy and dramatic force of the plays comes from that reality; and that issues of communication or non-communication in the plays derive also from the characters, who are not merely put on stage to voice or depict some theory of the author's own. Beyond that, Pinter will rarely be drawn. Harry Thompson, interviewing Pinter for the academic publication *New Theatre Magazine*, elicits important early statements about political drama, including one that he finds 'didactic and moralistic' theatre 'sentimental and unconvincing' (in transcriptions of Pinter's speech, the unobtrusive use of parallel clauses and adjectives is remarkable). Thompson also asks Pinter about the 'ballad-opera form' (as used by Brecht), alternative modes of theatre architecture, and questions of genre in his plays. These are issues that would have concerned an academic drama critic, expecting to place Pinter in the context of the theatrical avant-garde. Pinter is polite in his response, but clearly does not see his own work in that way.

By the 1970s Pinter was established as a major figure in British theatre. From 1973 to 1983 he served as Associate Director of the National Theatre, collaborating closely with the Artistic Director, Peter Hall. Despite the formidable workload demanded by this position, touching on all areas of policy and production, in addition to his work as writer and director, Pinter produced three major plays in the 1970s: *Old Times* (1971), *No Man's Land* (1975) and *Betrayal* (1978). The settings of the plays had shifted, in line with Pinter's own surroundings, from East London to the West and centre, and the characters were no longer derelicts, although class and social tension remain essential elements in the drama. The writing also had developed, emphasising more austere, lyrical and reflective elements of Pinter's talent. Influenced perhaps by his year of working on his *Proust Screenplay*, based on *A la Recherche du Temps Perdu*, Pinter explored increasingly themes of memory and time.

Roger Davidson's interview describes the experience of working at the National in a production directed by Pinter during this period. Pinter was only in his early forties, but was looked up to by almost all actors as a figure of tremendous seniority. Davidson recalls his mastery of theatrical craft, his sympathy and understanding for actors, and his quiet determination to concentrate on words, feelings and actions, rather than any extraneous theories in which a young actor might be caught up.

Pinter's new plays of the 1970s were all directed first by Peter Hall, whose interview is the longest in this book. Hall makes clear that he had strong views on the development of Pinter's work; views that became something of a dominant orthodoxy at that time. Hall suggests that it is his duty to push the work (sometimes even against resistance from audiences or the writer himself) towards its proper artistic destiny: an austere, difficult, and at times almost self-reflexive modernist refinement. Elements of comedy, plot, physicality and character seem to be lesser concerns, and in retrospect Hall's account of Pinter appears, perhaps, a little less authoritative and comprehensive than it may have seemed at the time. When Hall comments that *The Birthday Party* is not entirely 'free of being a rep play' he clearly means to observe a weak or underdeveloped aspect of Pinter's work at that time, where it might alternatively be argued that the way that play engages in a dialogue and struggle with the rep play is one of its most important and vital elements. It cannot be denied that Hall's approach was in line with some of the developments of Pinter's writing at the time, and it produced some great productions. But later interviews make it clear that attitudes to Pinter and the playing of Pinter have definitely shifted away from Hall's approach.

The notable contrast between the approaches of Hall and Sam Mendes illustrates some of the changes in Pinter playing over the years. As a director, Mendes is indubitably one of the natural successors to Hall in combining powerful productions with an evident intellectual seriousness, but in his interview he stresses the humour and the memorable lines in Pinter, and relishes the anarchic and comic elements of the plays; elements stressed in his own production of *The Birthday Party* for the National Theatre.

Peter Hall says little about the contemporary relevance of Pinter's plays. In retrospect, however, the work of the 1970s can be seen to reflect the time in which it was written almost as much as the earlier plays reflect the 'swinging sixties' with their social climbers, conspicuous consumption and sexual experimenting. In the plays of the 1970s Pinter examines images of English cultural life and identity which are viewed often through an acute sense of personal loss and a troubling, retrospective uncertainty. In terms of public politics, Britain in that decade saw a painful unravelling of the economic and governmental settlement which had, broadly speaking, endured since the Labour government of 1945; a settlement whose foundation Pinter and his friends had supported with passionate intensity. 1979 saw the election of a Conservative government that set about dismantling the mixed economy, close government links with trade unions, and a good deal of the Welfare State. *No Man's Land* negotiates with literary myths of England, especially the moral and political optimism of T.S. Eliot's wartime *Four Quartets*, and seems to see them as, at best, exhausted, or at worst, fraudulent. The play is saved from abject negativity by the humour and tenacity of the characters, and by its own formal authority and mature linguistic brilliance. Nevertheless, Spooner and Hirst emerge, albeit with pathos, as the mutually antagonistic remnants of a literary and intellectual culture that is creatively spent, historically belated and personally impotent. The span of the characters' reminiscences is from the 1930s to the contemporary – the period of Pinter's own lifetime – and the play offers a bleak assessment of what the nation has to show for those years. Written in the same period, the twin endings of Pinter's screenplay for *The French Lieutenant's Woman* offer Jeremy Irons and Meryl Streep romantic fulfilment and hope in the Victorian plot, but frustration and loss in contemporary Britain.

Interviewed by Harry Thompson in 1961, Pinter commented that Arnold Wesker's use of drama to comment on trade-union issues seemed to be 'happening on the other side of the moon'. However, it was under the immediate stimulus of a strike by stagehands at the National Theatre that he voted Conservative (later described in a considered and repeated phrase as 'the most shameful act of my life') in the General Election of 1979: the year when *Betrayal*'s study in English disillusionment and equivocation completed its first run at the National Theatre.

In 1980 Pinter married the writer Lady Antonia Fraser, whom he had met and, by his own account, fallen almost immediately in love with early in 1975. Interviewees and other friends of Pinter insist that this relationship has been vital to Pinter's remarkable productivity in the last two decades – a time during which it is said that Lady Antonia has rescued the manuscript of at least one of Pinter's plays from the wastepaper basket. Unlike Pinter himself, his wife has a background in public and political life, and she moves in such milieux with practised ease and a strong sense of entitlement. Through two decades in which Pinter has written and commented on politics both in the theatre and as a public figure respected by international news media, his wife has been conspicuous alongside him.

During the second term of the Thatcher government, Pinter began to speak out against British government policies, commenting directly on government and party politics in a way that he had never done before in public. He dated his sense of responsibility to speak out on political matters from the US government-sponsored overthrow of the Chilean government in 1973. Important interviews from this period are contained in this book. The plays from this period are his most explicitly 'political', addressing, in particular, issues of torture and freedom of speech. *One for the Road* (1984) is a series of scenes between an interrogator and members of a persecuted family. *Mountain Language* (1988) describes brutal physical and cultural persecution,

and *Party Time* (1991) juxtaposes a gathering of the privileged with one victim of torture. Critics have linked these
plays to Pinter's concern with world affairs, though this
perhaps overlooks their setting in Britain.

Throughout the 1990s Pinter continued to work and write
with remarkable energy. *Moonlight*, written in 1993, was his
first full-length play for over a decade. Where *No Man's
Land* drew extensively on T.S. Eliot, *Moonlight* draws on the
late work of the rejuvenated W.B. Yeats, as if to hint at a
second (or third) coming of Pinter's own dramatic writing.
Moonlight was followed by *Ashes to Ashes* in 1996, *Celebration*
in 2000, and a new sketch, *Press Conference* in 2002, and
flanked by major directing and acting work.

THE INTERVIEWS

The interviews in this book cover the period 1960-2001.
Those previously published date mainly from the 1960s to
the 1980s. Introductions to the individual interviews comment on their value in shedding light on Pinter and his
work, and on how the approach of the interviewer shows the
state of Pinter criticism and the terms in which his work was
discussed and understood at the time.

The new interviews, conducted in 2001, are with actors
and directors rather than journalists or critics. They discuss
the particular demands and rewards of playing Pinter, and
sketch an overview of his career from the differing perspectives of three generations of performers. All the new interviewees have at some stage collaborated with Pinter himself
in some capacity, and almost all are, or have been, friends of
Pinter.

The interview texts are distilled from transcriptions of
much longer conversations, usually of about two hours.
Substantial cuts were unavoidable, for reasons of space,
repetition and, in several cases, discretion. What remains is
a set of perspectives covering Pinter in the theatre from the
1950s to beyond the millennium, with practical comments

on the rehearsal and playing of the major plays and most of the major roles.

Henry Woolf, Susan Engel and Barry Foster are Pinter's contemporaries. They speak of his youth, early work in the theatre and the beginning of his career as a playwright. They also comment on major characters they have played.

Roger Davidson and Roger Lloyd Pack are about twenty years younger, and came to Pinter's plays as young actors encountering acknowledged contemporary masterworks. They speak of their own parts in Pinter's plays, of his influence on the British theatre in which they began their careers, and of being directed by him in his own and others' work.

Harry Burton, Douglas Hodge, Katie Mitchell and Sam Mendes are a generation younger. Paradoxically, when these artists came to the work in the mid to late 1980s, Pinter's great success in the 1960s and 1970s could almost have been seen as a hindrance. The problem they faced was almost the reverse of that faced by Engel, Foster and Woolf, who strove to persuade a sceptical public and critical consensus of the value and seriousness of the plays. Rather it was to bring freshness to material whose great success had deprived it of some of the alien and disturbing aura that had been central to its early impact. These artists' comments on specific plays and parts with which they have dealt offer insight into how they have triumphantly confirmed the durability and variety of Pinter's work.

Naturally, the artists often differed sharply in their interpretation of the plays and in their chosen theatrical methods. Roger Davidson recalls how his 'method' approach to acting was politely but comprehensively dismissed by Pinter the director at the National Theatre. Katie Mitchell, however, insists that 'method' work is the sole authentic approach to Pinter's plays. (When I asked how this would fit with Pinter's acknowledged brilliance as an actor in his own work, the reply, perhaps light-hearted, was that Pinter *is* a method actor, but just doesn't realise it.) Some interviewees emphasised Pinter's spontaneity, others the precision of his writing.

Harry Burton proposed that Pinter's writing was in touch with 'archetypal forces' in nature and the world about him.

For all these differences, however, many common views emerged. All the interviewees agreed in an emphasis on character, motive and plot in playing Pinter. Though they agree that elements of ambiguity or uncertainty are essential to the plays, the artists insist that a successful performance requires actors to develop the maximum certainty and consistency in their roles. This stress on people and actions goes against much early critical suggestion that Pinter's work is an expression of 'Absurdist' or other theories of drama or human life.

All stressed the importance of attention to the text. Though this might seem unworthy of comment to students, it is common practice in the theatre for the texts of plays to be trimmed; considerations of time alone dictate that the entire texts of Shakespeare plays are almost never performed. Reputations are made in the theatre by lending a distinctive turn to established texts, augmenting them with extravagant gestures, dramatic stage devices, innovative settings, costumes, etc. In Pinter, no speech can be altered without unbalancing the play, and actors believe that minor slips of the tongue or forgotten lines are more damaging to scenes in Pinter than in almost any other writer's work. Pinter believes that his career as a screenwriter has been restricted by his insistence that his name (which is prestigious and marketable) cannot appear on a film's credits if any change is made to the screenplay without his approval. The minute attention to language that results is not merely at the surface of the characters and actions. The artists insist that Pinter's characterisation is 'in the language', and in the pauses between words and actions which are meticulously specified in the texts. Actors must attend fastidiously to each word of their own character and to each action and word of their interlocutors. When asked by Joan Bakewell what he admired in Anew McMaster's acting, Pinter recalled not the magnificent voice, imperial command of the stage or physical metamorphosis described in the essay 'Mac', but rather the precision with which McMaster would handle a cigar in an Oscar Wilde play.

Actors also insist that in Pinter, the performer must have a strong sense of the shape of the play as a whole; an understanding of the structure and significance within which each different production and performance takes place. So it seems that in order for an actor to give a performance fully immersed in the individual role, the actor will ideally first have developed a critical sense of the play and its significance. Though all the interviewees insisted to me that their approach to the plays was practical rather than 'academic', almost all expressed strong views about Pinter's place in modern drama, the purpose of the theatre, and so on.

But theatrical performance retains its utterly paramount importance. Pinter as a writer and a man represents many different things to different people, but all those who know him seem to agree that if there is a centre to his identity it is as a 'man of the theatre'. Even by the standards of playwrights he has an unusually deep understanding of all aspects of the theatrical craft.

To an extent this picture given by his collaborators, of practical immersion in all the human range of dramatic life and work, is at odds with an image created by journalists and others of an austere and enigmatic writer fussing over the minutiae of his texts. In return, Pinter relishes the practical and collaborative processes of rehearsal and performance, and has the highest esteem for actors. As he says at the end of his interview with Miriam Gross: 'I . . . spend a great deal of my life with actors, and enjoy their company very much. I think the image of actors as children, narcissistic and vain, is quite inaccurate. They're very hard-working people, people with considerable imagination and intelligence on the whole. As a body of people, I respect actors more than I respect any other body. Oh yes, apart from cricketers.'

NOTES

1   June 1986, in Pinter's private archives. The other letters cited in this introduction are from the same source.
2   In conversation with the present author.
3   From Pinter's 'A Speech of Thanks' on accepting the David Cohen Prize, reproduced in *Various Voices*, Faber and Faber, 1998.
4   Ibid.
5   See Pinter's interview with Miriam Gross in this volume.
6   See Pinter's interviews with Lawrence Bensky and Anna Ford in this volume.
7   In conversation with the present author.
8   *The Sunday Times*, 25 May 1958.
9   See Goldstein's letter to Michael Billington in this volume.
10 See the interview with Barry Foster in this volume.
11 See Pinter's interview with Harry Thompson in this volume.
12 Statistics from Alan Sinfield (ed.), *Society and Literature 1945-1970*, Holmes and Meier, 1983.
13 The essay 'Mac' reproduced in *Various Voices*. See also the interview with Barry Foster in this volume.
14 Roger Davidson, in conversation with the present author.
15 From 'A Speech of Thanks' in *Various Voices*.
16 Ibid.
17 Ibid.

Pinter on Pinter

Harold Pinter Replies

Pinter interviewed by Harry Thompson
for *New Theatre Magazine*, II.2, January 1961.

*This early interview sees Pinter refusing to categorise his plays
and insisting that he writes to no preconceived plan or formula.
Writing for a journal published by the University of Bristol
Drama Department, Harry Thompson tries to link his work
to other work in the theatrical 'avant-garde' of the time – the
Brechtian ballad-opera form, the direct political comments of
Wesker and innovative methods of staging. Pinter politely
replies that these are not his own concern.*

*It seems at first sight that your plays might not meet with the
success more conventional plays enjoy. Have you any idea why
your plays have been so successful, particularly in the West End?*

No, I haven't. *The Birthday Party* did not succeed when put
on in London two years ago. Very possibly if *The Caretaker*
had been put on two years ago the same thing would have
applied. There has been some change of climate that I cannot define; some change in the theatregoing public itself, or
an adjustment of the public taste to certain developments in
the drama.

*The theatre itself would probably give a good deal to define
exactly what the shift in taste has been. In repertory there is a
great deal of uncertainty about what will go over. Do you agree
with what I have heard forcibly put, that there is a very clear
breach in requirement between the young members of an audience
and the older members?*

I haven't made a study of audiences. I am not a sociologist. Others may find it easy to break the audience up into its component parts; I don't. All I know is that some members of an audience are receptive to the work in hand and others are not. I don't think that whether they're young or old has much to do with it.

Do you try to visualise any particular audience when you are writing your plays?

No. None whatsoever.

There is in this country at the moment a revival of the ballad-opera form, as in The Hostage *and* The Tinker. *Has your mind turned in this direction?*

No, it hasn't. It doesn't appeal to me. I enjoy watching these plays but I don't think I shall ever turn to that form myself.

Do you oppose attempts to categorise plays – tragedy, comedy, tragi-comedy and so on?

Yes. I think these arbitrary distinctions are very stale by now.

Do you think in terms of categories at all when you consider plays?

No, I don't. This category business is the most facile of things. My only categories are plays that I like and plays that I don't. Most critics apparently are not able to view a play as it is by itself, distinctly and simply. They must relate it to what they saw last week or last year; usually this relation is tenuous, cock-eyed, unjust to both works. The critic is afraid to either sink or swim when he sees a play; he must grasp the lifebelt of a category.

Have you ever consciously looked to any other playwright for the sources of your work?

No, I certainly have not, but there is no question that Beckett is a writer whom I admire very much and have admired for a number of years. If Beckett's influence shows in my work, that's all right with me. You don't write in a vacuum; you're bound to absorb and digest other writing; and I admire Beckett's work so much that some of its texture might appear in my own. I myself have no idea whether this is so, but if it is, then I am grateful for it. However, I do think that I have succeeded in expressing something of myself.

One accepts that you reflect certain aspects of the time more closely than any other playwright, especially the hidden fears that seem to affect so many of us today. Are you yourself aware of such fears? Did you begin to write out of a sense of contemporary strains and tensions, or does your style come to you objectively, by observation?

The last thing I would attempt to do is to disassociate myself from my work, to suggest that I am merely making a study of observable reality, from a distance. I am objective in my selection and arrangement, but, as far as I'm concerned, my characters and I inhabit the same world. The only difference between them and me is that they don't arrange and select. I do the donkey-work. But they carry the can. I think we're all in the same boat.

Among playwrights, Arnold Wesker has made the problem of political conscience very much his own. Do politics interest you?

I find most political thinking and terminology suspect, deficient. It seems to me a dramatist is entitled to portray the political confusion in a play if his characters naturally act in a political context, that is, if the political influences operating on them are more significant than any other consideration. But I object to the stage being used as a substitute for the soapbox, where the author desires to make a direct statement at all costs, and forces his characters into fixed and artificial postures in order to achieve this. This is hardly fair on the characters. I don't care for the didactic or moralistic theatre. In England I find this theatre, on the whole, sentimental and unconvincing.

You say that your plays spring essentially out of a situation. Would you say your creative imagination was more visual than verbal? Have you any idea of the mental process that goes on when you are writing?

I see things pretty clearly, certainly, but I am continually surprised by what I see and by what suddenly happens in the play while I am writing it. I do not know, however, that the visual is more important to me than the verbal, because I am pretty well obsessed with words when they get going. It is a matter of tying the words to the image of the character standing on the stage. The two things go very closely together.

Do you think that you are conscious of a formula or of aiming at a formula?

No. I am aware that I was expected in some quarters to elaborate on my own formula. I did not see it as such, however, until I was told it was becoming one. Later I realised that in one short television play of mine there were characteristics that implied I was slipping into a formula. It so happened this was the worst thing I'd written. The words and ideas had become automatic, redundant. That was the red light for me and I don't feel I shall fall into that pit again. I trust that when I next fail it will be for different reasons. My basic approach to my work, anyway, is strongly opposed to such mechanism.

Have you in any way concerned yourself with the perennial debate about theatre architecture?

I have worked in various types of theatre – in theatre-in-the-round, with arena staging, but mainly, of course, with the proscenium theatre. I am not terribly bothered about new forms. I always think of the proscenium stage when I'm writing. I did produce *The Birthday Party* myself in the round, and it was a rewarding and worthwhile experience. This form has certain qualities the proscenium stage lacks, but I should say an equal number of limitations.

Do you find that your ten years' acting experience has conditioned your writing?

Yes. I write pretty meticulously, and when I write the last draft, I carefully work out the movements as I visualise them, and the pauses too. The thing must be capable of realisation, and it must work visually for me. If I feel something to be impossible visually, then I have to adjust it. I always write in direct relation to the visual image of people walking about and standing on the stage.

You played Goldberg in The Birthday Party *a few months ago at the Everyman in Cheltenham. How did this affect you?*

I found it a very difficult part to act and the lines hard to learn, but I enjoyed it tremendously, and I do not think I did too badly.

Have your scripts been modified much on the stage from their original form?

I do, of course, make various adjustments in rehearsal, which I am happy to do. In certain cases, however, productions of my plays have been highly unsatisfactory because of the difficulty of reconciling one's own intentions with those of a director, who will in many cases see the play very differently.

Do you prefer to direct your own plays?

No. I'm not very good at it. I find I concentrate too much on every minute detail and so the play tends to overrun by about an hour.

I find that your plays have a sense of cohesion – that the whole play hangs together and goes through on one note. Are you conscious of this?

I am very concerned with the shape and consistency of mood in my plays. I cannot write anything that appears to me to be loose and unfinished. I like a feeling of order in what I write.

Do you know soon after you have begun a play where it is likely to stop?

Not entirely. I have a pretty good idea of the course of events and I know whereabouts it must stop, but I very rarely know how it's going to stop. All the preconceived notions I have are invariably wrong, for they are remedied by the characters in the writing. At the end of *The Caretaker*, there are two people alone in a room, and one of them must go in such a way as to produce a sense of complete separation and finality. I thought originally that the play must end with the violent death of one at the hands of the other. But then I realised, when I got to the point, that the characters as they had grown could never act in this way. Characters always grow out of proportion to your original conception of them, and if they don't, the play is a bad one.

The Art of the Theatre

Pinter interviewed by Lawrence M. Bensky
in *The Paris Review*, 1966.

*A thoughtful and extensive account of Pinter's career to 1966.
The original introduction which follows gives an excellent
account of Pinter's manner in discussing his work, and of his
working environment.*

*Harold Pinter recently moved into a five-storey 1820 Nash house
facing Regent's Park in London. The view from the floor-through
top floor where he has installed his office overlooks a duck pond
and a long stretch of wooded parkland; his desk faces this view,
and in late October, when the interview took place, the changing
leaves and the hazy London sun constantly distracted him as he
thought over questions or began to give answers. He speaks in a
deep, theatre-trained voice which comes rather surprisingly from
him, and indeed is the most remarkable thing about him
physically. When speaking he almost always tends to excessive
qualification of any statement, as if coming to a final definition
of things were obviously impossible. One gets the impression – as
one does with many of the characters in his plays – of a man so
deeply involved with what he's thinking that roughing it into
speech is a painful necessity . . . Though [his new house] is not
yet completely renovated, the size and comfort of it are impres-
sive, as is Mr Pinter's office, with a separate room nearby for his
secretary and a small bar equally nearby for the beer and scotch
which he drinks steadily during the day, whether working or not.
Bookshelves line one half of the area, and a velvet chaise longue
faces the small rear garden. On the walls are a series of Feliks*

*Topolski sketches of London theatre scenes; a poster of the Monte-
video production of* El Cuidador [The Caretaker]*; a small
financial balance sheet indicating that his first West End production,* The Homecoming [sic]*, earned 260 pounds in its disastrous week's run; a Picasso drawing; and his citation when he
was named to the Order of the British Empire last spring. 'The
year* after *the Beatles,' he emphasises.*

*

When did you start writing plays, and why?

My first play was *The Room*, written when I was twenty-
seven. A friend of mine called Henry Woolf was a student in
the drama department at Bristol University at the time when
it was the only drama department in the country. He had
the opportunity to direct a play, and as he was my oldest
friend he knew I'd been writing, and he knew I had an idea
for a play, though I hadn't written any of it. I was acting in
rep at the time, and he told me he had to have the play the
next week to meet his schedule. I said this was ridiculous, he
might get it in six months. And then I wrote it in four days.

Has writing always been so easy for you?

Well, I had been writing for years, hundreds of poems and
short pieces of prose. About a dozen had been published in
little magazines. I wrote a novel as well; it's not good enough
to be published, really, and never has been. After I wrote
The Room, which I didn't see performed for a few weeks,
I started to work immediately on *The Birthday Party*.

What led you to do that so quickly?

It was the process of writing a play which had started me
going. Then I went to see *The Room*, which was a remarkable experience. Since I'd never written a play before, I'd of
course never seen one of mine performed, never had an

audience sitting there. The only people who'd ever seen what I'd written had been a few friends and my wife. So to sit in the audience – well, I wanted to piss very badly throughout the whole thing, and at the end I dashed out behind the bicycle shed . . .

What other effect did contact with an audience have on you?

I was very encouraged by the response of that university audience, though no matter what the response had been I would have written *The Birthday Party*, I know that. Watching first nights, though I've seen quite a few by now, is never any better. It's a nerve-wracking experience. It's not a question of whether the play goes well or badly. It's not the audience reaction, it's *my* reaction. I'm rather hostile towards audiences – I don't much care for large bodies of people collected together. Everyone knows that audiences vary enormously, it's a mistake to care too much about them. The thing one should be concerned with is whether the performance has expressed what one set out to express in writing the play. It sometimes does.

Do you think that without the impetus provided by your friend at Bristol you would have gotten down to writing plays?

Yes, I think I was going to write *The Room*. I just wrote it a bit quicker under the circumstances, he just triggered something off. *The Birthday Party* had also been in my mind for a long time. It was sparked off from a very distinct situation in digs when I was on tour. In fact the other day a friend of mine gave me a letter I wrote to him in nineteen fifty-something, Christ knows when it was. This is what it says, 'I have filthy insane digs, a great bulging scrag of a woman with breasts rolling at her belly, an obscene household, cats, dogs, filth, tea-strainers, mess, oh bullocks, talk, chat rubbish shit scratch dung poison, infantility, deficient order in the upper fretwork, fucking roll on . . . ' Now the thing about this is, that was *The Birthday Party* – I was in those digs, and this woman was Meg in the play, and there was a fellow staying there in Eastbourne, on the coast. The whole thing remained with me, and three years later I wrote the play.

Why wasn't there a character representing you in the play?

I had – I have – nothing to say about myself, directly. I wouldn't know where to begin. Particularly since I often look at myself in the mirror and say, 'Who the hell's that?'

And you don't think being represented as a character on the stage would help you to find out?

No.

Have your plays usually been drawn from situations you've been in? The Caretaker, *for example.*

I'd met a few, quite a few, tramps – you know, just in the normal course of events, and I think there was one particular one . . . I didn't know him very well, he did most of the talking when I saw him. I bumped into him a few times, and about a year or so afterward he sparked this thing off . . .

As an actor, do you find yourself with a compelling sense of how roles in your plays should be performed?

Quite often I have a compelling sense of how a role should be played. And I'm proved – equally as often – quite wrong.

Your wife, Vivien Merchant, frequently appears in your plays. Do you write parts for her?

No. I've never written any part for any actor, and the same applies to my wife. I just think she's a very good actress and a very interesting actress to work with, and I want her in my plays.

Did you go to a lot of plays in your youth?

No, very few. The only person I really liked to see was
Donald Wolfit in a Shakespearean company at the time. I
admired him tremendously; his Lear is still the best I've ever
seen. And then I was reading, for years, a great deal of
modern literature, mostly novels.

No playwrights, Brecht, Pirandello . . .

Oh, certainly not, not for years. I read Hemingway,
Dostoevsky, Joyce and Henry Miller at a very early age, and
Kafka. I'd read Beckett's novels, too, but I'd never heard of
Ionesco until after I'd written the first few plays.

Do you think these writers had any influence on your writing?

I've been influenced *personally* by everyone I've ever read –
and I read all the time – but none of these writers particularly influenced my writing. Beckett and Kafka stayed with
me the most – I think Beckett is the best prose writer living.
My world is still bound up by other writers – that's one of
the best things in it.

Has music influenced your writing, do you think?

I don't know how music can influence writing; but it has
been very important for me, both jazz and classical music. I
feel a sense of music continually in writing, which is a
different matter from having been influenced by it. Boulez
and Webern are now composers I listen to a great deal.

Do you get impatient with the limitations of writing for the theatre?

No. It's quite different; the theatre's much the most difficult
kind of writing for me, the most naked kind, you're so
entirely restricted. I've done some film work, but for some

reason or other I haven't found it very easy to satisfy myself on an original idea for a film. *Tea Party*, which I did for television, is actually a film, cinematic, I wrote it like that. Television and films are simpler than the theatre – if you get tired of a scene you just drop it and go on to another one. (I'm exaggerating, of course.) What *is* so different about the stage is that you're just *there*, stuck – there are your characters stuck on the stage, you've got to live with them and deal with them. I'm not a very inventive writer in the sense of using the technical devices other playwrights do – look at Brecht! I can't use the stage the way he does, I just haven't got that kind of imagination, so I find myself stuck with these characters who are either sitting or standing, and they've either got to walk out of a door, or come in through a door, and that's about all they can do.

And talk.

Or keep silent.

After The Room, *what effect did the production of your next plays have on your writing?*

I was completely new to writing for the professional theatre, and it was rather a shock when [the failure of the first production of *The Birthday Party*] happened. But I went on writing – the BBC were very helpful. I wrote *A Slight Ache* on commission from them. In 1960 *The Dumb Waiter* was produced, and then *The Caretaker*. The only really bad experience I had was *The Birthday Party*; I was so green and gauche – not that I'm rosy and confident now, but comparatively . . .

What was the effect of this adversity on you? How was it different from unfavourable criticism of your acting, which surely you'd had before?

It was a great shock, and I was very depressed for about forty-eight hours. It was my wife, actually, who said just that to me, 'You've had bad notices before,' etc. There's no question but that her common sense and practical help got me over that depression, and I've never felt anything like that again.

You've directed several of your plays. Will you continue to do so?

No. I've come to think it's a mistake. I work much as I write, just moving from one thing to another to see what's going to happen next. One tries to get the thing . . . *true.* But I rarely get it. I think I'm more useful as the author closely involved with a play: as a director I think I tend to inhibit the actors, because however objective I am about the text and try not to insist that *this is what's meant,* I think there is an obligation on the actors too heavy to bear.

Since you are an actor, do actors in your plays ever approach you and ask you to change lines or aspects of their roles?

Sometimes, quite rarely, lines are changed when we're working together. I don't at all believe in the anarchic theatre of so-called 'creative' actors – the actors can do that in someone else's plays. Which wouldn't, however, at all affect their ability to play in mine.

Is there more than one way to direct your plays successfully?

Oh yes, but always around the same central truth of the play – if that's distorted then it's bad. The main difference in interpretation comes from the actors. The director can certainly be responsible for a disaster, too – the first performance of *The Caretaker* in Germany was heavy and posturised. There's no blueprint for any play, and several have been done entirely successfully without me helping in the production at all.

Do you outline plays before you start to write them?

Not at all. I don't know what kind of characters my plays will have until they . . . well, until they *are*. I don't conceptualise in any way. Once I've got the clues, I follow them – that's my job, really, to follow the clues.

What do you mean by clues? Can you remember how one of your plays developed in your mind – or was it a line-by-line progression?

Of course I can't remember exactly how a given play developed in my mind. I think what happens is that I write in a very high state of excitement and frustration. I follow what I see on the paper in front of me – one sentence after another. That doesn't mean I don't have a dim, possible overall idea – the image that starts off doesn't just engender what happens immediately, it engenders the possibility of an overall happening, which carries me through. I've got an idea of what *might* happen – sometimes I'm absolutely right, but on many occasions I'm proved wrong by what does actually happen. Sometimes I'm going along and I find myself writing 'C. comes in' when I didn't know that he was going to come in; he *had* to come in at that point, that's all.

In The Homecoming, *Sam, a character who hasn't been very active for a while, suddenly cries out and collapses several minutes from the end of the play. Is this an example of what you mean? It seems abrupt.*

It suddenly seemed to me right. It just came. I knew he'd have to say something at one time in this section and this is what happened, that's what he said.

Might characters therefore develop beyond your control of them, changing your idea – even if it's a vague idea – of what the play's about?

I'm ultimately holding the ropes, so they never get too far away.

Do you sense when you should bring down the curtain, or do you work the text consciously toward a moment you've already determined?

It's pure instinct. The curtain comes down when the rhythm seems right – when the action calls for a finish. I'm very fond of curtain lines, of doing them properly.

Do you feel your plays are therefore structurally successful? That you're able to communicate this instinct for rhythm to the play?

No, not really, and that's my main concern, to get the structure right. I always write three drafts, but you have to leave it eventually. There comes a point when you say that's it, I can't do anything more. The only play which gets remotely near to a structural entity which satisfies me is *The Homecoming*. *The Birthday Party* and *The Caretaker* have too much writing . . . I want to iron it down, eliminate things. Too many words irritate me sometimes, but I can't help them, they just seem to come out – out of the fellow's mouth. I don't really examine my works too much, but I'm aware that quite often in what I write, some fellow at some point says an awful lot.

Most people would agree that the strength in your plays lies in just this verbal aspect, the patterns and force of character you can get from it. Do you get these words from people you've heard talking – do you eavesdrop?

I spend *no* time listening in that sense. Occasionally I hear something, as we all do, walking about. But the words come as I'm writing the characters, not before.

Why do you think the conversations in your plays are so effective?

I don't know, I think possibly it's because people fall back on anything they can lay their hands on verbally to keep away from the danger of knowing, and of being known.

Several years ago, Encounter *had an extensive series of quotations from people in the arts about the advisability of Britain joining the Common Market. Your statement was the shortest anyone made, 'I have no interest in the matter, and do not care what happens.' Does this sum up your feeling about politics, or current affairs?*

Not really. But that's exactly what I feel about the Common Market – I just don't care a damn about the Common Market. But it isn't quite true to say that I'm in any way indifferent to current affairs. I'm in the normal state of being very confused – uncertain, irritated, and indignant in turns, sometimes indifferent. Generally I try to get on with what I can do and leave it at that. I don't think I've got any kind of social function of any value, and politically there's no question of my getting involved because the issues are by no means simple – to be a politician you have to be able to present a simple picture even if you don't see things that way.

Has it ever occurred to you to present political opinions through your characters?

No. Ultimately, politics do bore me, though I recognise they are responsible for a good deal of suffering. I distrust ideological statements of any kind.

But do you think that the picture of personal threat which is sometimes presented on your stage is troubling in a larger sense, a political sense, or doesn't this have any relevance?

I don't feel myself threatened by *any* political body or activity at all. I like living in England. I don't care about

political structures – they don't alarm me, but they cause a
great deal of suffering to millions of people.

I tell you what I really think about politicians. The other
night I watched some politicians on television talking about
Vietnam. I wanted very much to burst through the screen
with a flame-thrower and burn their eyes out and their balls
off and then inquire from them how they would assess this
action from a political point of view.

Would you ever use this anger in a politically-oriented play?

I have occasionally out of irritation thought about writing a
play with a satirical point. I once did, actually, a play that
nobody knows about. A full-length play written after *The
Caretaker*. Wrote the whole damn thing in three drafts. It
was called *The Hothouse* and was about an institution in
which patients were kept: all that was presented was the
hierarchy, the people who ran the institution; one never
knew what happened to the patients or what they were there
for or who they were. It was heavily satirical and it was quite
useless. I never began to like any of the characters, they
really didn't live at all. So I discarded the play at once. The
characters were so purely cardboard. I was intentionally –
for the only time, I think – trying to make a point, an explicit
point, that these were nasty people and I disapproved of
them. And therefore they didn't begin to live. Whereas in
other plays of mine every single character, even a bastard
like Goldberg in *The Birthday Party*, I care for.

*You often speak of your characters as living beings. Do they
become so after you've written a play? While you're writing it?*

Both.

As real people you know?

[59]

No, but different. I had a terrible dream, after I'd written *The Caretaker*, about the two brothers. My house burned down in the dream, and I tried to find out who was responsible. I was led through all sorts of alleys and cafés and eventually I arrived at an inner room somewhere and there were the two brothers from the play. And I said, 'So you burned down my house.' They said, 'Don't be too worried about it,' and I said, 'I've got everything in there, everything, you don't realise what you've done,' and they said, 'It's all right, we'll compensate you for it, we'll look after you all right' – the younger brother was talking – and thereupon I wrote them out a cheque for fifty quid . . . I gave *them* a cheque for fifty quid!

Do you have a particular interest in psychology?

No.

None at all? Did you have some purpose in mind in writing the speech where the older brother describes his troubles in a mental hospital at the end of Act II in The Caretaker?

Well, I had a purpose in that Aston suddenly opened his mouth. My purpose was to let him go on talking until he was finished and then . . . bring the curtain down. I had no axe to grind there. And the one thing that people have missed is that it isn't necessary to conclude that everything Aston says about his experiences in the mental hospital is true.

There's a sense of terror and a threat of violence in most of your plays. Do you see the world as an essentially violent place?

The world *is* a pretty violent place, it's as simple as that, so any violence in the plays comes out quite naturally. It seems to me an essential and inevitable factor.

I think what you're talking about began in *The Dumb Waiter*, which from my point of view is a relatively simple piece of work. The violence is really only an expression of the question of dominance and subservience, which is possibly a repeated theme in my plays. I wrote a short story a long time ago called 'The Examination', and my ideas of violence carried on from there. The short story dealt very explicitly with two people in one room having a battle of an unspecified nature, in which the question was one of who was dominant at what point and how they were going to be dominant and what tools they would use to achieve dominance and how they would try to undermine the other person's dominance. A threat is constantly there: it's got to do with this question of being in the uppermost position, or attempting to be. That's something of what attracted me to do the screenplay of *The Servant*, which was someone else's story, you know. I wouldn't call this violence so much as a battle for positions, it's a very common, everyday thing.

Do these ideas of everyday battles, or of violence, come from any experience you've had yourself?

Everyone encounters violence in some way or other. It so happens I did encounter it in quite an extreme form after the war, in the East End, when the fascists were coming back to life in England. I got into quite a few fights down there. If you looked remotely like a Jew, you might be in trouble. Also, I went to a Jewish club, by an old railway arch, and there were quite a lot of people often waiting with broken milk bottles in a particular arch we used to walk through. There were one or two ways of getting out of it – one was a purely physical way, of course, but you couldn't do anything about the milk bottles – *we* didn't have any milk bottles. The best way was to talk to them, you know, sort of 'Are you all right?' 'Yes, I'm all right.' 'Well, that's all right then, isn't it?' And all the time keep walking toward the lights of the main road.

Another thing: we were often taken for communists. If you went by, or happened to be passing, a fascist's street meeting, and looked in any way antagonistic – this was in Ridley Road market, near Dalston Junction – they'd interpret your very being, especially if you had books under your arms, as evidence of your being a communist. There was a good deal of violence there, in those days.

Did this lead you toward some kind of pacifism?

I was fifteen when the war ended. There was never any question of my going when I was called up for military service three years later. I couldn't see any point in it at all. I refused to go. So I was taken in a police car to the medical examination. Then I had two tribunals and two trials. I could have gone to prison – I took my toothbrush to the trials – but it so happened that the magistrate was slightly sympathetic, so I was fined instead, thirty pounds in all. Perhaps I'll be called up again in the next war, but I won't go.

How much are you aware of an audience when you write?

Not very much. But I'm aware that this is a public medium. I don't want to *bore* the audience, I want to keep them glued to what happens. So I try to write as *exactly* as possible. I would try to do that anyway, audience or no audience.

There is a story – mentioned by Brustein in The Theater of Revolt *– that Ionesco once left a production of Genet's* The Blacks *because he felt he was being attacked, and the actors were enjoying it. Would you ever hope for a similar reaction in your audience? Would you react this way yourself?*

I've had that reaction – it's happened to me recently here in London, when I went to see *US*, the Royal Shakespeare Company's anti-Vietnam War production. There was a kind of attack – I don't like being subjected to propaganda, and I detest soapboxes. I want to present things clearly in my own plays, and sometimes this does make an audience very uncomfortable, but there's no question about causing offence for its own sake.

Do you therefore feel the play failed to achieve its purpose – inspiring opposition to the war?

Certainly. The chasm between the reality of the war in Vietnam and the image of what *US* presented on the stage was so enormous as to be quite preposterous. If it was meant to lecture or shock the audience I think it was most presumptuous. It's impossible to make a major theatrical statement about such a matter when television and the press have made everything so clear.

Do you consciously make crisis situations humorous? Often an audience at your plays finds its laughter turning against itself as it realises what the situation in the play actually is.

Yes, that's very true, yes. I'm rarely consciously writing humour, but sometimes I find myself laughing at some particular point which has suddenly struck me as being funny. I agree that more often than not the speech only *seems* to be funny – the man in question is actually fighting a battle for his life.

There are sexual undertones in many of these crisis situations, aren't there? How do you see the use of sex in the theatre today?

I do object to one thing to do with sex: this scheme afoot on the part of many 'liberal-minded' persons to open up obscene language to general commerce. It should be the dark secret language of the underworld. There are very few words – you shouldn't kill them by overuse. I have used such words once or twice in my plays, but I couldn't get them through the Lord Chamberlain. They're great, wonderful words, but must be used very sparingly. The pure publicity of freedom of language fatigues me, because it's a demonstration rather than something said.

Do you think you've inspired any imitations? Have you ever seen anything in a film or theatre which struck you as, well, Pinteresque?

That word! These damn words and that word 'Pinteresque' particularly – I don't know what they're bloody well talking about! I think it's a great burden for me to carry, and for other writers to carry . . . Oh, very occasionally I've thought listening to something, hello, that rings a bell, but it goes no further than that. I really do think that writers write on . . . just write, and I find it difficult to believe that I'm any kind of influence on other writers. I've seen very little evidence of it, anyway; other people seem to see more evidence of it than I do.

The critics?

It's a great mistake to pay any attention to *them*. I think, you see, that this is an age of such overblown publicity and over-emphatic pinning down. I'm a very good example of a writer who can write, but I'm not as good as all that. I'm just a writer; and I think that I've been overblown tremendously because there's a dearth of really fine writing, and people tend to make too much of a meal. All you can do is try to write as well as you can.

Do you think your plays will be performed fifty years from now? Is universality a quality you consciously strive for?

I have no idea whether my plays will be performed in fifty years, and it's of no moment to me. I'm pleased when what I write makes sense in South America or Yugoslavia – it's

[64]

gratifying. But I certainly don't strive for universality – I've got enough to strive for just writing a bloody play!

Do you think the success you've known has changed your writing?

No, but it did become more difficult. I think I've gone beyond something now. When I wrote the first three plays in 1957, I wrote them from the point of view of *writing* them; the whole world of putting on plays was quite remote – I knew they could never be done in the reps I was acting in, and the West End and London were somewhere on the other side of the moon. So I wrote these plays completely unselfconsciously. There's no question that over the years it's become more difficult to preserve the kind of freedom that's essential to writing, but when I do write, it's there. For a while it became more difficult to avoid the searchlights and all that. And it took me five years to write a stage play, *The Homecoming*, after *The Caretaker*. I did a lot of things in the meantime, but writing a stage play, which was what I really wanted to do, I couldn't. Then I wrote *The Homecoming*, for good or bad, and I felt much better. But *now* I'm back in the same boat – I want to write a play, it buzzes all the time in me, and I can't put pen to paper. Something people don't realise is the great boredom one has with oneself, and just to see those words come down again on paper, I think, oh Christ, everything I do seems to be predictable, unsatisfactory, and hopeless. It keeps me awake. Distractions don't matter to me – if I had something to write, I would write it. Don't ask me why I want to keep on with plays at all!

Do you think you'd ever use freer techniques as a way of starting writing again?

I can enjoy them in other people's plays – I thought the *Marat/Sade* was a damn good evening, and other very different plays like *The Caucasian Chalk Circle* I've also enjoyed. But I'd never use such stage techniques myself.

[65]

Does this make you feel behind the times in any way?

I *am* a very traditional playwright – for instance, I insist on having a curtain in all my plays. I write curtain lines for that reason! And even when directors like Peter Hall or Claude Régy in Paris want to do away with them, I insist they stay. For me, everything has to do with shape, structure, and over-all unity. All this jamboree in 'happenings' and eight-hour movies is great fun for the people concerned, I'm sure . . .

Shouldn't they be having fun?

If they're all having fun, I'm delighted, but count me out completely, I wouldn't stay more than five minutes. The trouble is, I find it all so *noisy*, and I like quiet things. There seems to be such a jazz and jaggedness in so much modern art, and a great deal of it is inferior to its models: Joyce contains so much of Burroughs, for example, in his experimental techniques, though Burroughs is a fine writer on his own. This doesn't mean I don't regard myself as a contemporary writer: I mean, *I'm here.*

Pinter on Pinter

Pinter interviewed by Miriam Gross, first published
in *The Observer*, 5 October 1980.

*This interview was given as Pinter approached his fiftieth
birthday, and took the form of a relaxed retrospective over his
life and career. The version here is edited, since much of it covers
material that is now well known and treats episodes that are
mentioned elsewhere in this volume. The distinctive feature of
the interview is the relaxed and playful tone that emerges,
showing a side of Pinter's character that interviewers often miss.
By comparison with later interviews, his political concerns are
less marked, and Pinter here seems ready, up to a point, to
accept his status as an established figure, and to respond by
presenting himself genially, even as something of an English
eccentric. The reluctance of some parts of the English theatre to
take up his recent plays evidently concerned him, but this was in
the context of an ever-growing international success. It seems
that he was enjoying life in the approach to his marriage to
Antonia Fraser, and in this month the couple threw a party
which many of his friends fondly, if hazily, still remember.
Miriam Gross drew from Pinter one of his most often-quoted
comments, on the relative merits of cricket and sex. What his
bride thought of this has never entered the public domain.*

*Did you go to the theatre much, or at all, when you were a child?
When did you first go?*

At about the age of fifteen. The first thing I saw was Wolfit's
company – *King Lear*, *Macbeth*. We were taken by my English

master, who was a very remarkable man. He died last year; a great shock, actually. We'd remained close friends. The theatre meant a lot to him and he took a few of us to see Wolfit, and that left a great impression. *Lear* particularly, which I saw six times. I couldn't stop seeing it.

Was acting your main interest at school?

No, not at all. Literature was my main interest, poetry – and sport, and girls. Those were the three things.

Did you start writing poetry yourself at about that time?

Yes, at about thirteen. Before that I wrote stories. And then I was very excited by the discoveries that one makes. I discovered and read Joyce very early on, and Eliot and Dostoevsky, Hemingway and Sartre, etcetera, etcetera. I had a pretty vigorous time with them all, I used to discuss them at great length with my friends.

Did you fall for them [girls] and develop crushes and so on?

Not 'them'. When you say 'them', plural, that's not the case. I did have a pretty strong association with a girl in my early teens. But anyway, it was all rather different then. There was this dark world of sex which took place in mists and rain, in alleys and on park benches under trees. I remember it with a very special fondness; I hope for the sake of the young that it still exists, somewhere. But the thing that really obsessed me was literature.

And was it literature, poetry, that led you on to drama?

No, I didn't think very much about the theatre then. I didn't read plays, apart from Shakespeare and some of the Jacobeans. In fact apart from Shakespeare, I can't remember the first time I saw an ordinary play. It must have been much later on.

I did go to RADA for a couple of terms, but I didn't get on very well there. I was quite out of my depth, really, with what I took to be the general sophistication, the knowing-ness about the place. I was pretty lost. The girl I mentioned just now was also at RADA, but in a higher class, and I'd lost her, too.

So what did you do, just leave?

I didn't quite just leave. Although I was unhappy there, I still had my own kind of stability. I actually faked a nervous breakdown – in order to keep the grant, you see.

How does one do that?

One trains oneself to become extremely white in the face. Then you have to speak in a very low voice, hardly heard, and walk very slowly, and be on the verge of tears. All this worked extremely well.

Did you let any of your friends in on this?

I did, but my friends didn't know precisely when I was go-ing to take the final step. And there was one quite extra-ordinary coincidence. It so happened that on the very day I was to have my last interview with the Principal of RADA, I was standing in the lobby, and two of my friends suddenly came in through the front door of the place and said, 'Hello, Harold, coming to Lord's?' And I whispered, 'In five minutes, I'll meet you round the corner,' and then I went in and spoke in my low voice, on the verge of tears, and everything went perfectly well.

The interview was to establish that you were a broken man?

Yes, and the Principal patted me on the back – he was a very nice man, I'm sorry I deceived him – and he wished me well, and then I had leave of absence, you see. I walked very slowly out of RADA, very slowly down Gower Street, round the corner into Store Street – lovely day, by the way – and there were my friends. I ran towards them and shouted, 'I'm free,' and we jumped on a bus and went to Lord's – it was one of the happiest days of my life.

What about your parents, did they think you were still at RADA?

That's right, I got up at the same time every morning and left the house. This went on for some months, and I simply wandered about London. Cups of tea, and libraries, cricket, and I had just enough money to keep me going. When I got home I used to make up stories about what plays I was acting in and so on.

Did you feel at all guilty towards your parents?

I was concerned about them, yes, but I had no alternative as I saw it. And I had a rather fruitful few months, mooching about.

It wasn't a kind of George Orwell down-and-out existence? Did you meet tramps and the kind of people you put into your plays?

No. I wasn't storing anything away. I wasn't thinking in that way at all. I was also a conscientious objector at the time, which rather complicated things. I spent half the time waiting for trials and tribunals.

Why exactly were you a conscientious objector?

I've always had a deeply embedded suspicion of political structures, of governments and the way people are used by them. I was determined not to be used in that way. I was quite prepared to go to prison – I took my toothbrush along when I went to court, I was quite ready – and I was fortunate to be fined instead. I had two trials and was fined twice. My father paid the fines; my parents regretted the whole thing enormously, but they stood by me.

Would you have been a conscientious objector in, say, 1939?

No, certainly not. The feeling I had about National Service in 1948 wouldn't have applied in the war. I felt very strongly about the war. And still do, if you see what I mean. After all, I wasn't a child by the time it ended; though I was when it began.

And how did you get back into acting after you'd left RADA?

Well, actually I did go to another drama school for about a year, the Central School, and that was okay. I had a certain ability of a limited kind as an actor, and I couldn't see any other way of earning a living; I couldn't face the idea of going into an office.

After the Central, I did some things on radio, and then I went to Ireland for two or three years to work with Anew McMaster, the last of the great actor-managers. He was a wonderful man. It was great work, but very hard. We did seven plays a week, mostly Shakespeare, and we moved about a lot.

Were you still writing through all this time?

Oh yes, I was writing quite a lot, a lot of poetry. The first poems of mine that were published were in *Poetry London* in 1950, when I was twenty. They accepted two of my poems and I was immensely pleased. But when I got the magazine and opened it, I saw that they'd actually mixed the two poems together – two verses of one were followed by two verses of the other, and vice versa. The poems were pretty obscure at the best of times, but this made them quite incomprehensible. Naturally I was very upset, but later on they reprinted them the right way round.

It's rather surprising, don't you think, that you hadn't thought of writing plays before, since so many of your themes seem to lend themselves much more to drama than to poetry – conflict, people struggling for dominance or waging a war of nerves. And there's a lot of violence in them. Do you tend to see life in these terms?

I never think about what I think about life. I myself prefer a quiet life. But that isn't quite what we are faced with, is it, either outside ourselves or within ourselves? While we're talking now, for example, people are locked up in prisons all over the place, being tortured in one way or another. I'm quite raddled with these kind of images, with the sense that these things are ever present. I have plenty of violence within me, and from a child I've lived in a world in which there has been more and more violence of one sort or another. It's as simple as that, I think.

For example, after the war – this is something which very few people are aware of now – there was a considerable amount of fascist activity in the East End of London. In 1945, after the war. In the streets round a Jewish club I used to go to, and around the Ridley Road market – there was a big fascist stronghold there – we used to bump into quite a few of the boys, you know, and we had a number of set-tos. It was really quite ugly. They used to beat up old Jews in the Dalston Junction area.

In many respects it was a perfectly lively, quite vigorous community down there, but when the night fell you never knew what you were going to meet. I've never understood how the fascists were given that kind of leeway.

Another feature of your plays is that so many of the characters seem to have guilty pasts, there's a sort of something-nasty-in-the-woodshed feeling about them.

[72]

Well, I don't think there can be anyone alive who doesn't carry around a load of junk in his head which is his past life, and other people's lives. When one looks back, one can hardly be complacent about anything that has happened in one's life. I suppose the characters in these plays are heightened examples of people walking around with this load, this burden of things ill done, things badly done.

I know you're a great admirer of Proust – you've written a screenplay based on A la Recherche *– and he, of course, was a writer obsessed with the past. But in many ways you seem complete opposites. Proust is tremendously analytical, he constantly explains characters and their motives, while in your plays there are very few explanations, lots of questions are left unanswered.*

Well, I wouldn't talk about Proust and myself in the same breath, but you obviously don't have to be the same kind of animal as the person you admire. Just because I don't go in for that kind of analysis in my own writing doesn't mean that I can't appreciate it in somebody else's work, particularly when it's Proust. And there are so many layers in Proust apart from the analysis – his marvellously precise visual sense, for example, which is quite staggering if you read him very carefully. Certainly I've never had a year like the one I spent working on the screenplay of *A la Recherche*. The thing about Proust is, finally, the weight of the whole damn thing and its unerring accuracy – it moves one deeply. In a way that Joyce, for instance, doesn't, although Joyce has always been my boy, from the word go. But Joyce is really much more of a comic writer, in my view.

One of the great themes in Proust, and in literature generally, is romantic or obsessive love. I may be wrong, but there doesn't seem to be much love of that kind in your plays.

I think I'll put on my dark glasses for this one. I think there's a good deal of love about in some of my plays. But love can

[73]

very easily go down the wrong path and be distorted as the result of frustration in all kinds of different ways. In *The Homecoming*, for example, the violence of the family towards their son when he comes back from America, using his wife to embody their own rage or spleen or whatever, comes about because they don't know where to put their love. I think there's a great deal of love in that play but they simply don't know what to do with it.

There's a lot of courtesy and formality in your plays as well as aggression. Is courtesy important to you?

Yes, I do think courtesy is worth paying attention to. As long as it's genuine, not the hollow kind one bumps into all along the line. But spontaneity is the thing, isn't it? Mind you, not the kind of spontaneity that leads Americans to call you by your first name without knowing you. They can throw that kind of spontaneity down the drain as far as I'm concerned.

Today, for example, a fellow phoned me out of the blue, he didn't actually call me Harold, but he almost did. He said he'd written me a letter some time ago, and had I got it? I remained quite silent and he stuttered on to say that it was about a symposium in Ohio in 1982 or something, which he was trying to get together, and how much he'd like me to take part, etcetera, etcetera, etcetera. Eventually I said, 'How did you get my telephone number? Who gave you my telephone number?' I really do resent this kind of intrusion.

What do you feel about the fact that you are going to be fifty this week?

I feel rather good about it. I'm quite fit. I'm finding life rather a lively business in my fiftieth year.

Do you think one changes very much as one gets older – becomes less intense, for instance?

I damn well hope I'm less intense now than I was when I was young. But I don't think one's feelings become any less strong, certainly not. In many ways, quite the contrary. They're sharpened, heightened as one grows older, one's sight becomes rather longer, which also means that you can spot a dud a mile off, something that's a posture rather than a true state of affairs.

Do you feel at all what traditionally people are supposed to feel, that you're becoming more conservative, that the country is going to the dogs and so on?

I certainly have strong feelings about values and standards. I think there is less appreciation of quality; things have become less serious – for obvious reasons, I would have thought. The world's in such a state of panic, so anxious to get through the day without one of those lovely missiles from Norfolk exploding. I think there's a great deal of nuclear panic about, without people recognising it or referring to it, and this dictates many attitudes – the quick buck, the quick poem, the quick song, the quick whatever you like. And this means that it's 'pop' which has come to dominate everything.

You've mentioned cricket more than once. Why does it appeal to you so much?

I tend to believe that cricket is the greatest thing that God ever created on earth.

Greater than sex, for example?

Certainly greater than sex, although sex isn't too bad either. But everyone knows which comes first when it's a question of cricket or sex – all discerning people recognise that. Anyway, don't forget, one doesn't have to do two things at the same time. You can either have sex before cricket or after cricket – the fundamental fact is that cricket must be there at the centre of things. To put my cards on the table, I must also say that cricket means England to me.

In what particular way?

Well, the first thing is that you play cricket on grass, and I know there are grasses all over the world, but it's not like English grass, you know.

No: I want to correct this: it doesn't finally matter about the grass or the horses looking over the hedge or the white clouds in the summer sky and all that. You can also play cricket in pouring rain, well, not pouring rain but terrible drizzle, on an awful ground with a miserable bar (the bar, of course, is one of the points of cricket) with bloody awful beer and terrible sandwiches, and, as I say, pissing rain which you still have to play in because it isn't pissing quite enough – in other words, a context which is quite displeasing, but the fact remains that whatever the context the overall activity is still a thing of beauty and the people taking part in it, believe it or not, are in a certain sense transformed by it. Although it's often full of bad humour and irritations and selfishness, I do think – and this is a very nineteenth-century view of it all – that the game of cricket is good for the moral fibre and soul of the people engaged in it.

To get back to your plays, do you enjoy seeing them performed?

On the whole, yes. But what I find rather interesting is that my last three full-length plays have hardly been performed at all in this country, outside London. My last play, *Betrayal*, for instance, has been produced all over the world in the past year – there have been twenty-three separate productions in West Germany alone – but so far only one English provincial theatre has put it on – the Haymarket Theatre, Leicester, where it's running at the moment.

You've written quite a number of screenplays, haven't you?

Yes, I enjoy doing them, particularly the last one I did, *The French Lieutenant's Woman*: it was a very difficult task but totally absorbing. I've seen a good deal of the shooting, and I really think it's going to be quite a film.

Do you go to the cinema much yourself?

When I was young a great deal of my life was spent at the cinema, but nowadays I almost never go. One of the reasons I don't go is that I find it difficult to sit among groups of people. I find it difficult to concentrate – the whispering, the chatting, the eating of the popcorn.

The real sin embedded in the cinema system is the packets in which they keep their chocolates and their popcorn. The poor bastards who have spent so much time trying to get it right, up there on the screen – there's an outrage inflicted on them by the splitting, the ripping of these packages. I feel I'm going to burst a blood vessel and you can't keep on saying, 'Shut up, shut up,' all the time. People don't know what you're talking about.

The last time I went to our local cinema to see a film I very much wanted to see, *Interiors*, I found it quite intolerable – the smell and the splitting of bloody popcorn all over the place – and I left. So I'm becoming a crusty old man after all.

One gets the impression that you are a rather solitary individual. Do you see yourself in that way?

No. I don't think so. Antonia Fraser and I have lived together very happily for five years and are about to marry. And I have a good many friends; I also spend a great deal of my life with actors, and enjoy their company very much.

[77]

You don't find them narcissistic, vain and so on?

Not at all. I think the image of actors as children, narcissistic and vain, is quite inaccurate. They're very hard-working people, people with considerable imagination and intelligence on the whole. As a body of people, I respect actors more than I respect any other body. Oh yes, apart from cricketers.

Radical Departures

Pinter interviewed by Anna Ford on *Omnibus*
(BBC TV), transcript published in *The Listener*,
27 October 1988.

*By this time, interviews with Pinter had become rare. Even rarer
were occasions on which he had made public comment on what
his writing was trying to say. During the eighties, however, he
had assumed publicly a number of political responsibilities. He
became active in PEN, the international organisation founded
to promote links between writers of all nations, and a member of
both Amnesty International and Arts for Nicaragua.*

Mountain Language followed One for the Road *in depicting
state and military torture and oppression in a recognisable,
though non-geographically-specific, contemporary setting. In
this interview he links composition of the play to a visit to
Turkey, where the government was supported by the United
States. Elsewhere, Pinter has related how he and Arthur Miller
were effectively thrown out of the US Ambassador's house when
they raised questions about this. Here, as elsewhere, Pinter insists
that the abuse of human rights is an increasing danger in
Britain as well as overseas.*

Why did you write Mountain Language?

It has a rather odd history, actually. In 1985 I went to Turkey
with Arthur Miller, on behalf of International PEN, to inves-
tigate the situation of writers in Turkey, which was pretty
deplorable in fact. It was a very vivid and highly illumi-
nating trip in a number of ways. One of the things I learnt

while I was there was about the real plight of the Kurds: quite simply that they're not really allowed to exist at all and certainly not allowed to speak their language. For example, there's a publisher who wrote a history of the Kurds and was sent to prison for thirty-six years for simply writing a history of the Kurds.

When I got back from Turkey I wrote a few pages of *Mountain Language*, but I wasn't at all sure about it and put it away; in fact I nearly threw it away but my wife persuaded me not to. I did nothing for three years with it and then, one day, earlier this year, I picked it up and suddenly wrote it. The springboard, in answer to your question, was the Kurds, but this play is not about the Turks and the Kurds. I mean, throughout history, many languages have been banned – the Irish have suffered, the Welsh have suffered, and Urdu and the Estonian's language were banned; the Basques' language was banned, you know, at various times.

Was this the first time that you'd come across this sort of oppression?

Well, the first time that I'd ever been in a place where I actually met people who had been tortured. But, as you know, torture and this kind of treatment not only tend to destroy the person suffering it, but the whole of his family. For example, one trade-union leader I met in Istanbul – a very distinguished man, by the way – had been very badly tortured. He was out of prison, and very shaky indeed, but his wife was actually mute; she's lost her power of speech altogether. I think she saw him in prison and hasn't spoken a word since.

Is Mountain Language *written to shock?*

I don't write in those terms. I have no aim in writing, other than exploring the images that come into my mind. I find some of those images really quite shocking, so they shock me into life and into the act of writing. The image is there and you attempt to express it. I was jolted by the images and by the state of affairs they refer to, which I think are serious facts most people prefer, understandably, to remain indifferent to, ignore, pretend don't exist. One thing when you meet people who've been through these appalling deprivations and assaults on their system, you realise that they're exactly the same as you and I. Just because, for example, they're three thousand miles away, a lot of people say, 'Oh well, why don't we look at England?' Well, we are looking at England. By which I mean, 'Do not ask for whom the bell tolls, it tolls for thee.'

There's a lot of obscenity in the play. For example, the sergeant uses the word 'fuck' a lot, and then, towards the end of the play, Sarah says, 'Can I fuck him?'

It seems to me that those old Anglo-Saxon words are still very strong – they can hit you in the stomach – and I think the sergeant, who has a stick which he doesn't have to use, uses the words instead in a way. He's using it as an adjective, and she uses it as a verb. My understanding of what she's doing is that she's saying, 'This is the only practical world to inhabit, is that what you're saying? That if I do this, if I fuck this man you say can help me, then everything will be all right, will it?'

She doesn't get an answer.

She does. 'Will everything be all right?' she asks, and he says, 'Sure, no problem.' She says, 'Thank you.' She's not really going to do it, if you see what I mean. She's saying, 'Is that the only thing that is understandable, that is comprehensible to you – if I went through with a thing like that, would you treat my husband better?' It's a very crude, brutal world that she's entered into, and I think she's having a very tough time, but she despises it so thoroughly that she's able to use that language with no trouble at all. She's also tough.

There's a discussion with the sergeant about whether intellectual arses wobble more than other arses. Is this important to the play?

Yes, very; it's meant to be offensive. The sergeant puts his hand on her bottom, and she has to bear this. She's a dignified and intelligent woman, but she has to bear it for a few minutes. It's done under considerable threat. Finally, she moves away very easily, simply and purposefully, and defies them, merely saying that she wants to see her husband. She ignores it – doesn't scream or faint or do anything, just ignores it. I admire her very much. Seeing this act of control on her part, they discuss her arse as it were, in those terms, merely to offend, to attempt to find a chink in her, which they do later on in the play.

Mountain Language *is very short for a play – it's only twenty to twenty-five minutes long. Why is it so short?*

One way of criticising this play, possibly, is to say it's too short to express the subject, that the play cannot address itself seriously to such a subject at that length. Well, I would argue that that is not the case in this play, simply because I hope that the play has its own life.

Would you hope that people come away from the play thinking about relating Mountain Language *to what's going on in this country?*

I hope audiences will perceive it in their own way and make up their own minds. I haven't written a theoretical piece of work. It's not an ideological piece of work, either. In a sense, it's hardly political. It's simply about a series of short, sharp brutal events in and outside a prison. Whether that prison in that location and what actually takes place is at all recognisable as being possible in this country is up to any individual member of an audience to make up his own mind about. I believe it's very close to home.

As in many of your plays, a lot of the expression of violence in Mountain Language *is what is going to happen and what might happen. Is this one of the strongest forms of menace that you find it effective to write about, the use of language in this way?*

I've been writing plays for thirty years and many of them have to do with that mode of operation – of terrorising through words of power – verbal power, verbal facility. In *The Birthday Party*, I think it's most evident. I was a boy in the last war, you know, and the sense of the Gestapo was very strong in England. They weren't here, but we as children knew about them.

Were there discussions at home about what was going on in Germany?

Oh yes. We knew that the German force was a very strong one.

Did you know about concentration camps?

Not until 1945, when they were discovered. We now know that people in Whitehall knew and we know what they said about it – 'They were the whining Jews' – when they were told what was taking place.

You're a Jew.

I am, yes.

What do you feel about that sort of reaction?

Considerable anger.

[83]

Were you aware of anti-Semitism in the East End when you were growing up?

Oh God, yes, absolutely.

What form did it take?

Well, it took a violent form.

They had meetings, didn't they, in the East End. Did you keep away from them?

No, not at all. In fact I had a number of fights, but also one learnt how to avoid the fights by various means – by words, in fact.

You were a conscientious objector when you were eighteen. Did that get you into trouble?

Yes, it certainly did. It was a very unpopular thing to be, but it was 1948 and I must make clear that if I'd been older in the war, I would have definitely accepted military service.

So what was the difference between fighting in the Second World War and being an objector afterwards?

An enormous difference. At the tribunals it was the thing to bring a Reverend along – in my case it would have been a Rabbi – and then you could get off.

On what grounds?

Well, on religious grounds – pacifism. I didn't do any of that. I simply said I disapproved of the Cold War and wasn't going to join the Army in order to help it along as a boy of eighteen. But this irritated all the colonels on the bench. They asked, 'What would you do if your sister was raped?'

I haven't got a sister, but I said if I had a sister I would certainly defend her to the best of my ability. They said, 'But we thought you were a pacifist.' 'No, I never said that, I simply said I'm not going to subscribe to the Cold War.' I really did think very clearly about the millions of people who had been killed in the war, the war to end wars, and the tragic farce of starting the Cold War almost before the hot war had finished.

It's confrontational to put yourself in a position where people have the legal right to put you in prison. It's my experience that once you've been in that sort of direct political action it changes you as a person. You're becoming more and more political: is this going to affect your work and change your work?

Well, I think it has changed my work. My earlier plays are much more political than they seem on the face of it.

Did you recognise that? You've been interviewed before and you've said, 'No, I was not political at all and they are not political plays.'

Yes, I did recognise that, but I think that the plays like *The Birthday Party*, *The Dumb Waiter* and *The Hothouse* are metaphors, really. When you look at them, they're much closer to an extremely critical look at authoritarian postures – state power, family power, religious power, power used to undermine, if not destroy, the individual, or the questioning voice, or the voice which simply went away from the mainstream and refused to become part of an easily recognisable set of standards and social values.

But you do not interpret them as political plays?

Yes, I do.

Then you moved into a different period in which you wrote a number of plays that were blatantly not political. What happened then?

I think I was still well informed about what was going on in the world, but I had a tendency to treat the world of politics with what I can only describe as a detached contempt. I'm not terribly proud of that. I don't think it was very useful either for me or for anybody else. Meanwhile, I was watching more and more violations of human dignity with, as I say, a detached contempt, saying, 'Look, there they go. They're still doing it, they're not going to stop doing it,' but doing nothing about it myself.

You say that Mountain Language *is not specifically about the Kurds, or about their situation, although that's what prompted you. Wouldn't it be more useful if it was specific, so that people could tell exactly what was happening there?*

Well, I'm not writing a play simply about Turkey; in fact the play isn't about Turkey at all. I think the play is very much closer to home and I believe it reflects a great deal what's happening in this country.

What sort of things?

Well, my own view is that the present [Conservative] government [under Margaret Thatcher] is turning a stronger and stronger vice on democratic institutions that we've taken for granted for a very long time. It's embodied in things like Clause 28, the Official Secrets Act, police powers, and it's happening quite insidiously, but happening nevertheless in a very strong and purposeful way. I believe most people don't seem to realise that the dissenting voice and the minority are in great danger in this country.

So there's a parallel between the suppression of language in your play and the suppression of speech or language?

Well, speech – in other words, thought.

[86]

Can you give me an example of the suppression of speech or thought?

Clause 28 is a first example. Under it, the promotion of homosexuality will be against the law, in certain circumstances, through local councils. What it will encourage is censorship at all levels, certainly in public libraries and, I imagine, censorship in local theatres, in local cinemas. Apart from that, it seems to me that it's quite interesting that the homosexual is being seen as an alien force, something to be feared and therefore to be rejected and repressed. There are many other examples of repression growing in this country. One is the police's powers. In the miners' strike, if you recall, a lot of miners' supporters, driving out of Kent to Nottingham, were stopped by the police and turned back. It was actually asserted that the reason for this was they were intent on breaching the peace. Judgement was passed upon them without any trial or any investigation.

The other day the Turkish President came to Victoria Station, an official guest. At the station there were quite a few Kurds and a number of Turks who are exiled, with banners asking him to go away. Before the train arrived at Victoria Station, a number of them were taken by the scruff of the neck and thrust against the wall by the police – spread-eagled, the usual thing – and were kept there physically. They hadn't done anything. The police horses were very close to them, so they were covered in horse excrement during all this. You wouldn't expect when we talk about merry old England that this kind of thing happens. When the Conservatives came to power, one of their platforms was that they wanted to save the country from state control, those nasty socialists, the Labour Party centralising everything. What has actually taken place is that no state power has ever been stronger in this country.

So do you think we're going back to a new form of censorship and repression?

Yes, I do. I think it very often takes the form of self-censorship and out of fear of not being seen as one of the boys, fear of losing your job, and so on, and so on. For example, people are fighting very hard to defend the independence of universities, but I don't think it's going to be a very easy battle at all for those defenders to win.

What is happening to universities, do you think?

Well, any professor, shall we say, is now in a much more slippery atmosphere, much more of a quicksand than he ever was before, for the simple reason that if he is teaching something which the government considers to be unpopular – I'm putting it very simply here – or of which the government does not approve, funds gradually will be withdrawn.

Do you see other institutions being controlled in any way?

Well, I think that television's under considerable stress, and the press, of course, is in a very interesting state because most of it is more or less owned by about two people. Those two people are on the right side according to the government, and therefore their newspapers are pretty meaningless and so distorted and unbalanced as to be worthless.

So you don't see this as a free press any longer?

Just. There are one or two examples of the free left, undoubtedly.

You're a founder member of something called the 20th June Society.

What it is, is simply a group of serious independent people who decided to meet privately one night to discuss the state of the country.

People like John Mortimer, Margaret Drabble, Salman Rushdie . . . It met with a fair amount of ridicule in the press shortly afterwards. Were you surprised by that?

Yes, derision was used, and it struck me, of course, that derision, I'm sure you'll agree, and mockery are the staple weapons of the British establishment and always have been, and I must say, I find that kind of complacent malice and self-congratulatory spite quite simply beneath contempt.

You were called Bollinger Bolsheviks. Is this symptomatic of the fact that it now appears to be almost against the law to be in opposition in this country?

Yes, I think it is. What is really so sad is that these silly attacks came from so many people in the press who are part and parcel of the structure, and don't realise the extent to which they have been sucked into a very finally debilitating, insidious and corrupt state of affairs.

[89]

Writing, Politics and *Ashes to Ashes*

Pinter interviewed by Mireia Aragay and Ramon Simo, Universitat de Barcelona, Departament de Filologia Anglesa i Alemanya, 6 December 1996.

What does writing mean for you?

I was always extremely excited by language from a very early age. I started writing when I was eleven or twelve. I loved words as a child, and that excitement has remained with me all my life. I still feel as excited now as I ever did about words on a page and about the blank piece of paper and the words that might fill it. Every piece of blank paper is an unknown world which you're going to dive into. That is very challenging.

In 1961, in a conversation with Richard Findlater which was subsequently published as 'Writing for Myself', you stated that 'I start off with people, who come into a particular situation. I certainly don't write from any kind of abstract idea.' Has your creative process remained the same over the years?

Yes, I've never written from an abstract idea at all. It isn't so much necessarily specific characters as specific and concrete images, either visual or verbal.

Even in your more recent political plays, is that the way you go about writing?

Yes, even in my more recent *overtly* political plays. If you're going to write a play about these states of affairs, you've got to have an impulse, and the impulse must come from a

[90]

specific image. For example, *One for the Road*, which I think has been given a splendid production [here in Barcelona] at the Sala Beckett, began in my mind with a man sitting at a desk waiting for someone to come into the room, his victim. The image of the man sitting at the desk was the concrete fact that started the play. It wasn't the idea that started the play, it was the image of the man that got it going.

When discussing your creative process, you never mention planning or preconceived structures, yet your plays are formally extremely precise. Could you comment on how these two aspects co-exist in your work?

The formal construction is in the course of the work on the play. I still find that I have to construct very precise forms; it's part of the way I was born. I have the impulse, and then I have to organise that impulse and make it coherent. That coherence is to do with how you shape the language and the structure of the play, quite obviously. I take a great deal of care to do that. So the two things coincide; one is part of the other. I've got an animal in the middle of the play which has to be held by the author. But I like the animal, by the way. If it wasn't for the animal, there'd be nothing there at all.

How do you try to solve the aesthetic and ethical difficulties inherent in the writing of political plays? How do you avoid preaching to the audience, becoming a kind of prophet?

It *is* a great trap in writing political plays as such if you know the end before you've written the beginning. I have tried to avoid that and find it afresh, and I hope I'm not sermonising. I like to find what the state of affairs is and just let it happen. *Party Time* is a case in point. I started with the idea of a party in a very elegant and wealthy apartment in a town somewhere. It became clear as I was writing it that outside in the streets something else was happening. Gradually it became even clearer that what was happening in the streets, which was an act of repression, had actually been organised by the people in this room. But the people in the room naturally never discussed it, just one or two fleeting references. They were drinking champagne and eating canapés, and they were very, very happy. They knew that it was all going well. In other words, there was a world which didn't actually bother to discuss the acts of military and police repression for which they were responsible. This emerged during the course of the play. I was quite excited by that, in that it never became really very explicit, but it was as clear as a bell, I think. Without making any great claims, I believe it's an image that has a universal reference. I believe that there *are* extremely powerful people in apartments in capital cities in all countries who are actually controlling events that are happening on the street in a number of very subtle and sometimes not so subtle ways. But they don't really bother to talk about it, because they know it's happening and they know they have the power. It's a question of how power operates.

The general feeling across Europe now, among playwrights and people involved in the theatre generally, is that political theatre is quite an impossibility.

Political theatre now is even more important than it ever was, if by political theatre you mean plays which deal with the real world, not with a manufactured or fantasy world. We are in a terrible dip at the moment, a kind of abyss, because the assumption is that politics are all over. That's what the propaganda says. But I don't believe the propaganda. I believe that politics, our political consciousness and our political intelligence are not all over, because if they are, we are really doomed. I can't myself live like this. I've been told so often that I live in a free country, I'm damn well going to be free. By which I mean I'm going to retain my independence of mind and spirit, and that I think that's what is obligatory upon all of us. Most political systems talk in such vague language, and it's our responsibility and our duty as citizens of our various countries to exercise acts of critical scrutiny upon that use of language. Of course, this means that one does tend to become rather unpopular. But to hell with that.

Brutality and the obvious are always present in your political plays. Aren't these two elements limiting when it comes to discussing politics?

My plays are not political discussions. They are living things. They are certainly not debates. They *are* violent. Violence has always been in my plays, from the very beginning. *The Room* ends with a sudden, totally gratuitous act of violence on the part of a man who kicks a negro to death. I was quite young at the time, but looking back it doesn't seem to me to be a wild or bizarre thing. We are brought up every day of our lives in this world of violence.

What's the aim of building such brutal, obvious images in your political plays?

There's no aim. I do not have an ideology in my plays. I just write; I'm a very instinctive writer. I don't have a calculated aim or ambition; I simply find myself writing something which then follows its own path. And that path tends to include acts of violence of one kind or another, because it is the world in which I live. And so do you.

Brutality and violence are often related to the male characters in your plays, whereas the women, especially in the plays you wrote in the 1960s, are enigmatic, mysterious, they have a kind of staying power which the men don't seem to have.

They also tend in later plays to be victims of male brutality.

Don't you think those are rather stereotypical views of men and women?

Possibly.

[93]

Do you stand by them?

I think that men are more brutal than women, actually. There's a terrible two-line poem by Kingsley Amis, in which he says, 'Women are so much nicer than men / No wonder we like them.' My wife considers these lines to be very patronising, and they certainly are, I quite agree. But nevertheless, I just believe that God was in much better trim when He created woman. Which doesn't mean to say I sentimentalise women. I think women are very tough. But if you look at what has happened in the world since day one, the actual acts of brutality have been dictated by men. Sometimes they have been exercised by women, that is certainly true. In the German camps the women did fine from that point of view; they really fulfilled what was asked of them as men, or rather it didn't matter; they were hardly women, they weren't men, they were just people acting for their state, for their God. Nevertheless, in my plays women have always come out in one way or another as the people I feel something towards which I don't feel towards men.

That's a very male point of view, isn't it?

Why not?

There is a lot of violence in your plays, but there is also a great deal of humour, as you reminded us last night at the Sala Beckett.

Humour is part of my own upbringing. I don't write what I call funny things, but some of them do make me laugh. I find myself laughing while I'm writing and I notice one or two people also laugh, occasionally.

I was surprised on the opening night of Ashes to Ashes *in Barcelona to hear the audience laughing. When I read the play it didn't seem to me to be dealing with anything particularly funny.*

Yes, there *are* some laughs in *Ashes to Ashes*. But I think they stop. The comic, in a way, is the best of what we are. I don't think I write very cruel funny things; I think I write quite affectionate humour, although it can be pretty terse and critical. But on the whole, the laughter goes out of any play I've written before it's finished. I can't think of any play of mine in which there are really any laughs at all in the last ten minutes. But it's not calculated; it's instinctive.

Last night at the Sala Beckett, the audience laughed during the performance of One for the Road. *Do you think that is an adequate reception of the play?*

That depends. I'd be very surprised to find that they laughed in the scene between Nicolas and Gila. But there *are* other laughs. We also laugh when we recognise the ugliness of people, the ugliness in ourselves. It's very much a question of recognition of our own worst characteristics. So I've actually contradicted myself. I've said laughter is created by true affection; it's also created by quite the opposite, by a recognition of where we are ugly.

According to Simon Gray, in One for the Road *you are also on the side of Nicolas somehow. Now you said many years ago, in relation to* The Birthday Party *and* The Homecoming, *that you didn't love or hate any of your characters more than any other. Would you make the same point in relation to your political plays, such as* One for the Road?

I'm not terribly fond of Nicolas; I could do without him. Nevertheless, I recognise the plight he's in. Don't forget Nicolas is a deluded man; he's a man possessed, religiously, really. He's enacting a religious and political obsession, and I feel very sorry for him. He's an absolute disaster, but the society he's speaking for is in itself a disaster. Coming back to that old cliché – but it's a cliché based on absolute evidence – he will go home to his wife and children, and listen to music, as is touched upon in the production at the Sala Beckett – the music, absolutely right. That the torturers listen to music and are very kind to their children has been well established throughout twentieth-century history. This is one of the very complex states of affairs in the psychology of our social and political lives. I have no answer to any of these; I'm just tapping.

In 'Writing for the Theatre', the speech you delivered in 1962 before the National Student Drama Festival held at Bristol, you defended the self-sufficiency of art by claiming that, 'What I write has no obligation other than to itself.' Do you still hold that view or has it been modified in any way?

I still essentially feel the same as I did then. I feel that my first obligation is to the work in hand. What I was really talking about when I said that was that I don't feel I have any obligation or responsibility to my public. The public will always do whatever it does. But I have a responsibility towards the text. For example, *Old Times* and *Betrayal*, are not in any sense political plays; they've no political life, they're about other things. But I feel the same responsibility to those plays as I do to my more political plays. So my first responsibility, whatever the nature of the play, is always to the play itself. What I mean is I won't be budged; I won't ever change a play once it's written.

Is that the reason why over the years you have come to direct several of your own plays? Do you think the playwright is the only legitimate interpreter of his or her own plays?

No. I really enjoy seeing what other directors do with my plays.

As a director, you're often described as very meticulous, and yet you speak of the danger.

It's the same thing as I was asked about my writing plays; I hope I'm both spontaneous and meticulous, you can be both things at the same time. There's a line in *Party Time* about death being both quick and slow at the same time; I think directing plays can be quick and slow at the same time. The whole point about directing plays and engaging with plays – I'm sure every actor here will know this out of their own discoveries – is that you don't know where you're going, but you've got to find out, and then when you find out, you don't know what the next step is going to be either. But it's very important not to collapse on the stage and say, 'I don't know where I'm going'; you've got to keep your feet, but it's very precarious.

You do enjoy acting, don't you?

I've been an actor all my life. I started in school when I was sixteen. Then I became a professional actor when I was nineteen. I was very, very fortunate because I was plunged into a world of Shakespeare in Ireland with the great actor-manager Anew McMaster and I played in *Hamlet, Othello, Oedipus Rex, Julius Caesar, King Lear*, one night after the other. We played several nights a week in Irish villages. I was twenty at the time and I could take it. It was a very rich existence, and I was introduced into this whole Shakespearean world too, which was wonderful.

How should actors deal with your plays? When they ask you about the underlying motivations of your characters, you often answer, 'Just do it.'

Alan Ayckbourn tells this story which I don't really believe is true. I directed him in *The Birthday Party* when he was an actor in 1959. He did say to me, when I first met him, 'Can you tell me where this character comes from, where he lived, who his parents were?' I just said, 'Mind your own business. Just do it.' But I don't really believe that I said that because these are perfectly legitimate questions for an actor to ask. The trouble is I can't answer all that many of them. I literally do not know what some of my characters were doing the day before yesterday. I've always felt, and that's what makes writing very exciting for me, that I meet these characters having not known them before. I don't plan them at all, I don't write any literature about them to myself; I just find them, and therefore I have to find out about them.

Could you tell us what prompted you to write Ashes to Ashes?

Ashes to Ashes is about two characters, a man and a woman, Devlin and Rebecca. From my point of view, the woman is simply haunted by the world that she's been born into, by all the atrocities that have happened. In fact they seem to have become part of her own experience, although in my view she hasn't actually experienced them herself. That's the whole point of the play. I have myself been haunted by these images for many years, and I'm sure I'm not alone in that. I was brought up in the Second World War. I was about fifteen when the war ended; I could listen and hear and add two and two, so these images of horror and man's inhumanity to man were very strong in my mind as a young man. They've been with me all my life, really. You can't avoid them, because they're around you simply all the time. That is the point about *Ashes to Ashes*. I think Rebecca inhabits that.

The obvious question is, is it a play about Nazism?

No, I don't think so at all. It *is* about the images of Nazi Germany; I don't think anyone can ever get that out of their mind. The Holocaust is probably the worst thing that ever happened, because it was so calculated, deliberate and precise, and so fully documented by the people who actually did it. Their view of it is very significant. They counted how many people they were murdering every day, and they looked upon it, I take it, like a car delivery service. How many cars can you make in one day, how many people can you kill in one day? And there's the whole question of how many people knew what. In the recently published *Hitler's Willing Executioners*, Daniel Goldhagen claims that the majority of the German public was well aware of what was happening. It's certainly true, for example, that in the early days when they were killing people by gas in trucks, the engineers had to work out a way to do it that was practical and effective. These trucks weren't doing very well because they were lopsided, so that when the gas started to go in, people would rush to the back of the truck, which could fall over. They had to readjust the structure of the truck so that people would be killed without bothering the driver. This firm of engineers is still going very strong today; it's actually a great car empire in Germany. This also applied to many other people, like the people who made the gas. They weren't making it for killing chickens. But it's not simply the Nazis that I'm talking about in *Ashes to Ashes*, because it would be a dereliction on my part to simply concentrate on the Nazis and leave it at that. Again, as I try to say in the article I published in *The Guardian* on Wednesday, it's not simply that the United States, in my view, has created the most appalling state of affairs all over the world for many years, it's also that what we call our democracies have subscribed to these repressive, cynical and indifferent acts of murder. We sell arms to all the relevant countries, do we not? Not just the United States, but also Great Britain, France, Germany *and* Spain are very active in this field. And they still pat themselves on the back and call themselves a democracy. I wonder what the term 'democracy' actually means. If you are a democracy and you help people of other countries murder their own citizens, then what are you doing? What is that? What *is* that? What does it mean? I really don't understand how the United States can regard itself as a democracy just on the basis that it has elections every five years, if it also keeps 1.5 million people in prison and also possesses, the most barbaric of all things, the death penalty in thirty-eight states out of fifty. The death penalty has been abolished more or less all over the world, while our most enlightened democracy, the leader of what is usually called the free world, kills people in thirty-eight states, including young people under eighteen and mentally deficient people, by gassing them, electrifying them, by lethal injection. Or take England; in England now, the general political philosophy is to punish and to attribute blame and guilt to the innocent victim. One of the guilty elements in our society is the unmarried mother or single parent, and there are many of them. They are, in the main, dispossessed and alone, helpless and bewildered, treated by men casually and with no regard for their welfare. *They are treated with equal disregard by the state.* The single mother becomes a guilty person and welfare is taken away from her. We have many more beggars on the streets now than we've had in years, and many of them are single mothers with babies. I don't call that particularly democratic. The word democracy begins to stink. These things, as you can see, are on my mind. So in *Ashes to Ashes* I'm not simply talking about the Nazis; I'm talking about us and our conception of our past and our history, and what it does to us in the present.

Both the audience's and the critics' reception of Ashes to Ashes *was much warmer here than it had been in London. The actors and you yourself said you were much more pleased with the audience's reaction here than in Britain. What was the difference?*

What we appreciated here was the fullness of the response, the intelligence, and more than that, the willingness to enter into the play, to be part of it. The world we've been encouraged to inhabit in London is a world of cynicism and indifference, so many people – there were, of course, people who did listen, and did the same thing as happened in Barcelona, but they were really a minority – simply refused to listen, and what they did was cough.

What about the critics?

The critics didn't cough, I think. In London, both publicly and critically, it was a much more spasmodic experience. In Barcelona it was a much fuller experience, and I was very happy to be here.

English critics and the English press have generally been rather hostile to your work in recent years, especially after you became publicly involved in political affairs.

In Britain there is no tradition of artists being respected; artists are actually *not* respected. Nor is there a tradition of artists being in any way engaged in politics, as there is on the Continent. There's also a very deep-seated tradition of mockery; mockery is the one thing they can still keep going. It comes easily for the English people to mock. It's a very odd situation indeed in England; you try to address real facts of life that surround you and are treated with great hostility.

When you organised the June 20 Group, with your wife and other writers and intellectuals, you were indeed treated with great animosity.

We started the group simply to question the appalling situation we found ourselves in in England under Mrs Thatcher's regime, which was destroying so many institutions and convictions that we thought were really part of the essence of England. We were being given another thing altogether, which was that the essence of England was, as I said, punishment, and making money. Mrs Thatcher, I remind you, said immortally: 'There is no such thing as society.' One of her really great statements. And she meant it. She meant by it that we have no obligation or responsibility to anyone else other than ourselves. This has encouraged the most appalling greed and corruption in my society. For example, recently electricity has been privatised in a number of different constructs, procedures and bodies. The people who found themselves owning the electricity companies sold them to someone else for 27 million pounds. These twelve directors walked away with 27 million pounds, whereas old-age pensioners and the poor, of whom there are more and more and more, can hardly pay the electricity bill. That, I find, is an extraordinarily corrupt use of power; it's totally cynical. In the 1980s, through the June 20 Group, we were drawing attention to this kind of thing in no uncertain terms, but we were undermined finally by the hostility generally surrounding us, and the thing collapsed.

Was it a form of censorship, in a way, on the part of the media?

It *is* a brilliant form of censorship, but then it's not actually censorship, it's just derision. If you have derision day after day after day, you think, I give up. But that was a weak moment on our part, certainly on *my* part. I no longer feel that way. I feel no sense of giving up, and I believe there are many people in my country who feel the same thing. The only trouble is that we have an opposition, the New Labour Party, as it calls itself, which desperately wants to become the government. This is almost certainly going to happen, because people have been nauseated by the Conservative government over the last seventeen years. But in the meantime, the Labour Party has allowed some very bad bills to become law without any protest whatsoever because they simply don't want to rock the boat. This is an absolute disgrace, in my view. For example, the Police Bill is going through Parliament at this moment. It will legalise police bugging of private houses. MI5, the secret service, has this provision too, but they have to go to the Home Secretary for permission. But the police need only go to the Chief Constable and say, 'We're going to do this to him, him, him, her, her, her.' And the general application will by no means be restricted to terrorists or criminals; it will actually apply to people who go on strike, people who write letters to the papers, like me, and all dissenting voices. In other words, it means that the police can do exactly what they like. I think that this is an appallingly undemocratic law, but it has been agreed by the opposition. The Prevention of Terrorism Act has recently come to the same thing. There's a big IRA problem, and has been over the years, there's no question about that. But nevertheless, this Prevention of Terrorism Act means that anyone could be stopped on the street for no reason at all, simply at a policeman's whim. He will simply ask the person to show him his wallet or open her handbag. If the person refuses, she's under arrest, and can be given six months in prison. On Monday morning, when I get back from here, I'm going to the trial of a friend of mine who was one of forty-one people who simply sat down a couple of months ago outside an arms trade conference in London as a peaceful protest, doing no harm at all, but simply regis- tering their disapproval. They were all arrested. I believe this kind of thing masquerades under the terms democracy and freedom. I'm not saying that Britain is a totalitarian country. I'm saying, however, that there are totalitarian measures which countries which call themselves democracies can easily employ. The British Parliament was once called, by a Conservative in fact, an 'elected dictatorship'.

You're saying that there's no opposition left in Britain; is there any Left left in Britain, or in Europe?

There's a little bit of Left left in Britain. I pray that there is a Left left in Europe, but we have to recognise that the forces against the Left are very great and very ruthless. By the Left I also mean, incidentally, the poor. It seems to me the poor have become the real enemy of the rich. They always have been, but now it's being embodied in concrete terms. Now the communists are no longer in operation as a worldwide force, the poor have become the new force of subversion, because they do affect the stability of the state.

So the only thing to do with the poor is keep them poor. Nicaragua, which I was very, very close to in the 1980s, is a case in point. The Sandinista Revolution, in my opinion and my observation, was a really serious, responsible, intelligent, thoughtful and concerned action. It was inevitable, it happened; and what they then did was to cultivate and establish social systems in Nicaragua which had never been seen before. I'm talking about health and education, literacy, doing away with disease; actually bringing people back from the dead, giving them life. People who'd been totally poverty-stricken all their lives. This was a really responsible act, which was then totally destroyed by the United States. And this has gone under the blanket. It's as if it never happened, but it *did* happen. And one has to keep drawing attention. I find what the Sandinista Revolution was doing was really valuable, important, and *civilised*. If I sound possibly very pronounced in my views about the United States, some might say over the top, I believe that what I'm saying is based on actual facts and actual states of affairs.

What is your relationship with your own Jewish identity?

I was never a religious Jew. The last religious subscription I made, the bar mitzvah, was when I was thirteen, which is a long time ago now. That's the last time I was in a synagogue, apart from one or two weddings and one or two funerals. I've no religious beliefs whatsoever, but I'm still Jewish. I don't know what that means, really, nobody ever does. But what I know it does not mean is that I subscribe to what is happening in the state of Israel. I deplore what is happening in Israel, and I've made my position very clear. Not as a Jew, but as a citizen, as a man. For example, I'm a trustee of the Vanunu Estate; he's been in prison for over nine years now in solitary confinement and he has another nine to go, for simply reporting on the Israeli nuclear capability. I've been to the Israeli embassy in London many times in this connection. When my mother was alive, she certainly didn't like that at all. But, of course, my mother and father belong to a different generation; I understand why they felt so strongly that you couldn't criticise Israel, because they were brought up in the 1920s and 1930s. But I'm not in that position. Again something that's happening under cover is the detention camps that still exist in the West Bank, in the Sinai desert. Palestinians are still in prison in detention camps, many of them without charge at all. I think this is really appalling, and I think the last election in Israel was a disaster. I believe there may be real civil unrest over there because it's really a fifty-fifty thing.

In your Guardian *article you also talk about memory, about the way it is manipulated by power, by the media. How can the ordinary person fight this process and not be engulfed by it?*

That is precisely the point, indeed. The terrible thing is that the media is now used politically all over the world. There is such a relationship between the media and the people in political power that it's very difficult to see any distinction between one and the other. This is certainly the case when you look at television. Television all over the world now is more or less run by about three people, as far as I can gather. You switch on any given news programme and see precisely the same thing in the Sahara desert as you do here and in London, because there is a central control. In other words, that news is highly selective and very specifically controlled . . . the words Rupert Murdoch are not far from my lips, I have to say. But it's not just Rupert Murdoch. In England now, our opposition, which might very well become the next government, has made great friends with Rupert Murdoch. They've done that because he has a kind of power that they want to lock into. That's a very corrupt state of affairs. It all comes down to: power is money and money is power. That's a cliché which you know as well as I do, but it nevertheless does remain the case in so many really repulsive ways. What I find very dispiriting is how the controls that are in place all over the world have really undermined people to a terrible extent, for very practical reasons. Only recently, in England, I was talking to some people about this kind of thing; it was very much a university audience. A man got up and said, 'Now look, I agree with what you're saying, but I'm a lecturer at Cardiff University, and I couldn't possibly say this myself publicly.' Somebody else said, 'But you're not saying you'd lose your job?' And he said, 'No, I don't think I'd lose my job, but I would not be promoted.' This is an extraordinary and very horrifying curb on free speech, in what we call a democracy, by the way. You asked what can the man on the street do. I think what we can do, since we're all men and women of the street, is simply to keep it right there [*touches his forehead*] and try to articulate it.

Voices from the Past

Mick Goldstein

Letter written to Michael Billington in 1984.

Mick Goldstein is one of Pinter's oldest and closest friends. He was an important model for the character of Len in the novel and play The Dwarfs, *and the collection of plays* Other Places *is dedicated to him. He now lives in Sydney, Australia, and when I suggested a telephone interview about his memories of Pinter's early days he offered to send the following letter, which he wrote to Michael Billington in 1984.*

Thank you for your letter. It would of course be much better if we had an opportunity to talk about Harold and the past over a schooner or two of beer, however I shall try to supply the information that you request as best I can. Didn't Martin Esslin undertake something similar in 1970 in *The Peopled Wound*?[*] But I don't suppose he had the opportunity of making contacts with people such as Henry or myself, even had he wished to do so.

There is much room for my representing the early years in Hackney with an exaggerated idealism and with a golden and mellow nostalgia. Be that as it may.

Meeting Harold again on my trips to London in the last few years is always a kind of return to the purity (I would say) of those times in Hackney and a renewed appreciation of the remarkable qualities of the man, whom I knew as a boy and

---

[*] Reissued as *Pinter the Playwright*.

who continues to evoke in me the choking sensation of
being burdened by ever-quickening time, ever-losing time.
Yet I think you are right when you talk about the fun,
liveliness and companionship amongst us. I do not think, in
recollection, that anyone of Henry Woolf, Moishe Wernik,
Jimmy Law, Ron Percival, or Harold himself had or claimed
any leading role, including, of course, myself! I rather think
that I had doubts as to my contribution to the discussion
which inevitably took place about anything and everything
that might have been artistically or politically topical at the
time. Whether it was about the question of Tynan's qualifi-
cations to call himself a drama critic, or whether it was an
evaluation of the newest performance of Gielgud or Donald
Wolfit. I was, personally, content to observe and listen and
learn. Someone would always rise to the surface and assume
perhaps a kind of leading role simply as a result of his better
understanding of the subject being discussed. Where it came
to drama, I think everyone (except me) had something important to say; in the realm of film, I think Harold generally
assumed the ascendant; if the subject was music or mathematics, I would feel I had something to contribute. In English
literature or poetry, Jimmy, Ron or Henry would provide a
point of departure; Moishe seemed always to occupy the
role of 'piss-taker' and no one could really get over-pom-
pous or over-serious. Except Ron who had a sharp tongue
and could generally give as good as he got – and he used to
'get' quite a lot and could be 'got at' frequently. By the way,
I should mention that Ron Percival had a kind of classical
almost Grecian beauty, quite delicate really. He was strik-
ingly fair skinned with long golden hair. Harold was also
very handsome – dark and powerfully built. They seemed
naturally to be fated to stand on either side of some
imaginary demarcation. It would be false to say that any one
of us was permanently in the ascendant.

To come to some of your questions; my first meeting with
Harold is quite unforgettable. I was supposed to meet a

bloke called Stanley Mendelssohn for a game of cricket
(just the two of us) over Millfields in Clapton. He had a bat,
and I had a ball and four stumps. He failed to appear, and
looking around I noticed a figure leaning on a cricket bat
under a large chestnut tree (or was it a beech?). In any case
I made contact and we were soon joined by at least two
more boys, whom I assume Harold had been waiting for,
from Hackney Downs School. I think their names were Brian
Kirkwood and John Gates. Pinter had a short-handled
Wisden bat, I think, but I'm not sure about that. In any case
when I came to bat, Harold was bowling from quite a long
run and he bowled one just outside my off stump which I
timed to perfection through the covers 'for four'. The next
ball took my off stump with an in-swinging yorker. I cannot
remember what I thought at the time, but it must have
made an impression, because very soon after that, just the
two of us were setting up the stumps and batting and bowling to each other, sometimes even when there was a thin
layer of snow on the ground. Much later when I started
work we still continued to have our 'cricket matches'. I used
to come off a shift as a continental telephone operator at
Faraday House near St Paul's, at seven o'clock in the morning and in quite poor light we would suddenly become
Hutton receiving Lindwall, or Miller taking guard to D.V.P.
Wright. Very rarely Henry, Moishe, Ron or Jimmy would
join us. We both listened to the early-morning radio cricket
commentaries which meant getting up very early. This went
back to 1946. We would quite often go to Lord's for the
opening match of the season, if Yorkshire were playing the
MCC, which they often were, as winners of the county
cricket championship. Hutton opening with Halliday (and
later Lowson) was always a tense moment. Pinter had a
tremendous feeling for Hutton's superb batting. It seemed a
tragedy whenever he was out. Being a supporter of Middle-
sex, I was stuck with Compton and Robertson, whom I
would never abandon, but I must say that I was jealous of
Harold's superior taste in the evaluation of the greater

aesthetic qualities of Hutton, Hardstaff, etc. I can remember this aspect of our love of cricket very clearly. I think Harold must have been surprised that I did not know of Neville Cardus. It was about this time that he lent me *The Summer Game* and I immediately got all his books out of the Hackney Public Library. And then I discovered that he was also the music critic on the *Manchester Guardian*. The point I wish to make is that Harold was responsible for introducing me to such authors as Hemingway, Henry Miller, James Joyce, Kafka, Chekhov, Shakespeare and much later, Samuel Beckett. A kind of education in English literature which I never had at school. Where did he discover these; who introduced these authors to Harold? He must have had a kind of sixth sense whether someone's writing was to his purpose or not, after reading a couple of sentences, I suppose. My efforts in English at school were so bad that I came to despair of doing a good composition and did not look forward to my English lessons. Moishe Wernik was in my class at Raine's Foundation School in Whitechapel, and he was always getting good marks for his essays. My writing at that time was very wild – undisciplined – and one of the criticisms that Harold got from those of the group who fancied themselves as decent literary critics was that his writing was also undisciplined. His poetry was very wild.

You mention Henry Woolf and Moishe Wernik. Well, I knew them both before either of them met Harold. I knew Moishe, from my school, before he joined Hackney Downs School in 1946-7 (because Raine's did not have an Arts sixth) and Henry in 1939 when we were both evacuated to Upwell – a village in the Fens – where we attended the same elementary school. Soon Henry got a scholarship to Hackney Downs School and left. So Henry, apart from my own family, is the person whom I have known the longest (since 1939) and we still correspond. Raine's Foundation School specialised in the sciences, and so I went into the Science sixth where I concentrated on Physics and Maths. So of 'our group,' I was perhaps the only one who had both a practical and aesthetic appreciation of mathematics.

But returning to the question of undisciplined poetry, there is one character called Jimmy Law, who lives in Sussex and who was, until last year, head of the English department at Worth School. He was one of 'us' at the time, together with Ron Percival (of *The Dwarfs*). I believe that Jimmy was often critical of Harold's lack of rhyme or metre and what he considered Harold's lack of discipline. There were quite often discussions on modern poets with Harold sticking up for Dylan Thomas, Ezra Pound, while others found them rather untidy as poets, etc. I kept well clear of any of these discussions. In fact, most of the time I was disinterested in talking about things but preferred to read or listen at first hand. I must mention that Harold was a prime mover in getting us to join him in seeing the foreign films that were being shown at that time. There was one memorable time when we went to see Buñuel's *Un Chien Andalou* at the Imperial College film society. How he knew these things were on I do not know. But if he said it was worth going to see, we went. Also Harold was a great admirer of the French cinema as a whole and we went to see Jean Gabin in *Le Jour se lève*, *L'Atalante* and many other French films. These were being shown at The People's Palace in Mile End Road and there were always crowds to see them; you had to queue for hours to get in.

In those days Harold would 'disappear up the West End'. If anyone knew where he went, it was certainly not common knowledge. I think on one occasion he tried to tell me that he had a female cousin who was 'on the game,' and whom he visited. But I did not take much notice. He would, before going home, call in to my place for a late-night cup of tea and a biscuit, since I lived just round the corner. I was usually up doing my home-work when there would be a knock on the door at around eleven at night or later. We would talk about this and that. I'd probably tell him about my readings of Bertrand Russell, Alfred North Whitehead and Wittgenstein and the general philosophical topics that were related to my mathematical studies. The philosophical or logical foundations that supported mathematical axioms such as that one and one makes two. A concept that I did, at that time, find genuinely not that obvious (and which, incidentally, I still have my doubts about). I also remember going on about the effect that late Beethoven quartets had on me. I believed Harold's musical sensitivities were fairly ordinary. I was intent on trying to persuade him of the power of this chamber music. I once got him to come to one of the South Place Sunday concerts in the Conway Hall in Red Lion Square, where I had a season ticket. He came with one of his girl friends of the time (I can't remember her name) and sat through what must have been a boring time for him for he never came again. Jimmy Law, on the other hand, attended these concerts quite frequently. We used to meet there. But in any case, I think I persuaded Harold that there was something vital in those concerts. I remember sitting just in front of Neville Cardus at a performance of Beethoven's Opus 127 and reading about it in the *Guardian* next day. The critique seemed to have nothing to do with the notes but everything to do with the power of the emotions that the notes carried to Cardus's inner ear. At one of these late-night tea tastings, I recall Harold quoting Cardinal Newman to me about the Creation being a vast aboriginal calamity. I never forgot this phrase, because it seemed that beneath the surface of our talk lay the empty, gaping black hole which, for me, Schubert (and Beckett) were familiar with. In the group as a whole we joined together at the Hackney Boys' Club and wherever else, like The Swan pub in Upper Clapton Road, and then we went our separate ways. We definitely had our separate lives and the meetings we had were an unselfconscious continuation of that. No one dominated to my recollection. It is, however, true to say that Harold had a uniquely strong character, with a definite if undefined (indefinable?) attitude to things.

I think we were interested in any philosophical topics and the various schools of philosophy were always a subject for discussion. I mean, the use of 'the necessary and the possible' in *The Birthday Party* may well have been a spin-off from these discussions. God came into it a lot with R.V. Percival having quite a bit to say about the origins of Christianity! I don't think we took anything quite as seriously as he did. It is my impression that we all regarded Harold as very special in his intense likes and dislikes. I am still aware of how careful Harold is about the language, and how a clumsy expression, which can distort what it is one wants to say, can turn him right off. In some ways the style of language – the words you choose – were as important as the meaning of what you wanted to say. This is something I had a very sensitive 'nose' for. I mean, in our quite regular correspondence when he was with the McMaster company in Ireland, I would use cricket terms to write about matters which were not at all about the game. I might write that 'the wicket is breaking up and the game is now in the balance' – or words to that effect, without the slightest doubt that I would be understood. And the same would go for him. The matter in hand would be the subterranean world of what unknown events lay in wait. If you like, it was as if the Dwarfs were making a report on their observations, from their vantage points in the corners of the room, while I was writing – biting their nails, picking their noses and licking their lips. Kafka knew all about this world too, I'm sure. It seemed that the use of this elusive type of language gave a clear emotional description of where we were without the specific revelation of our inner selves, which I think we were rather jealous of, or at least did not feel like revealing, even if we could. The truth of the matter might have been that perhaps only a woman could assuage the deep feeling of being alone in the world, which would be a common enough feeling, at our age, I suppose. But this is all post-facto surmise.

In Hackney, yes, you're right, there was an undercurrent of anti-Semitism, but by no stretch could you say that it was felt more than skin-deep by any of us. It was not a subject which received undue emphasis, unless there was an incident that involved one of us. Of course it was mentioned now and again, but I can't personally see how it informs Pinter's work to a great extent. There is enough fear and menace in just being alive. Do you go up to your neighbour and ask him, even politely, to turn his hi-fi down, or do you just throw a brick through his window? Well, if you ask whether this period represents an irretrievable past, in a sense it does. However much I muse over it, so much of that time is beyond recall. It is a misty past. On the other hand, as I have said, hardly a day passes without something jerking me back to that past. I read Pinter's work now with an intense longing to re-enter that world of Hackney and relive some of those priceless moments. Some of these moments, of course, I would want to eschew.

When I was knocked to the ground after coming out of Hackney Boys' Club (of which we were all members), the rest of us were naturally concerned, but the matter was soon forgotten. There were so many other more important things to get on with. There were a couple of occasions which I think Harold has already spoken about in interviews with John Kershaw in the sixties for ITV. Henry, Harold and myself were leaving the club very late and we were quickly aware that we were being followed by a gang of maybe seven or eight thugs carrying all sorts of things like chains and broken bottles. I can remember Harold, who was between me and Henry, saying quietly and confidently, 'Don't look back, just keep walking.' Then I broke ranks and ran to a police phone box across the main road, which we had nearly reached. I rang the police and after a while nothing happened so I returned home. Harold, who lived with his parents in an adjoining street to mine, had gone home, picked up a stout walking stick, and he and Henry had returned to look for me. They came back to my house where, of course, having already returned, I was safe. Another such incident occurred in Ridley Road (near the junction of Balls Pond Road – yes, it's still there). We had decided to attend a meeting of the British National Party (or whatever they were called at the time) and Jimmy was carrying a book under his arm (probably a volume of Baudelaire) when he was suddenly pointed at and accused of being a Commie, at which B.J. Law held his book aloft and called out, 'Why – because I can read?' Of course, we thought this was very funny. We left the scene followed again by a similar group as in the previous encounter. Harold trailed the others (Henry, Moishe and Jimmy) by some yards. They had already turned the corner into Dalston Lane when an enormous onion hit the wall of the bank we were just passing in Kingsland Road. I grabbed Harold by the arm to lead him quickly to catch up with the others, but he shook me off and turned to face the thugs. I ran to the others and called out that Harold was in trouble. By the time we got back to him he was surrounded by about six of them. Some of them had bike chains, others carried broken milk bottles. Jimmy broke into the ring and took up a position next to Harold. I think this was a very brave thing to do. At that moment a trolleybus slowed down to take the corner and all of us managed to scramble on. It was a nasty situation.

I always regarded Jimmy as intellectually head and shoulders above everyone else in that group, and I must say ever since then I have had a very special regard for Jimmy Law and after Harold's marriage to Vivien (I think this event, to which we all paid homage at a pub in Soho, was the watershed), it was not Moishe or Henry that I continued to see when the group split up, but it was Jimmy. He used to drink regularly in The Castle in Holland Park (it was a decent pub, in those days) – Charrington's best IPA. He had a great liking for music and in particular Schubert and other German lieder. And we could always go back to his place

and listen to some music after a bellyful of beer. Well,
I played violin and am now leader of my own semi-
professional string quartet. Sorry for this digression. But
Harold, after his marriage, had other matters to occupy
him. There was always a great sense of fun among us. This
was the predominating feeling. It was propelled by Moishe's
great ability to invent the most pointed quips and to reduce
quite serious matters to an absurdity. He had a spontaneous
talent for humour. Jimmy and Henry, too, but a more
rounded and perhaps more subtle kind of humour. Yet still
demolishing the presumptuous posturing that we could see
in the political and other important figures of the day.
Moishe's reference to Harold's supposed sexual prowess was
an example. He would say that all Harold had to do if he
wanted to go to a fancy-dress ball was hang his 'youga'
(Yiddish) over his shoulder and go as a petrol pump.
Phrases like 'farting Annie Laurie down a key hole', or 'from
arsehole to breakfast time' were standard repertory. To hear
these phrases nearly always caused me to have a near rup-
ture, to send me into a laughing fit. It is useless to try to
recall the effect these phrases had on me now, since then, I
was hearing them for the first time! I could appreciate
Harold's use of the type of language that would result from
the occasional distortion of using nouns, adjectives and
verbs indiscriminately. It was possible to invent a completely private language. I am not saying that I immediately
understood what it was that was being said, but there was a
lack of concern if the meaning of a phrase eluded one's
attempt to interpret it, provided that it had a life of its own.
The Dwarfs is full of such language.

It was many years later (after Harold's marriage) that I
found that Henry had written so many wonderful poems.
Harold had them published, I believe, at his own expense;
just as years earlier he had offered to pay for my violin
lessons when it was apparent that I could no longer afford
them. But he had no money then, in any case! On one

occasion he needed to borrow a tie from me. In a memorable exchange, I took him upstairs to my bedroom, opened a drawer which was full of ties and drew out a bright orange and black one which I offered to him. 'Too flock' was his immediate response. On that occasion I burst into uncontrollable laughter; but there were times more often when it was tears. On that occasion I became aware of a word which can evoke so much, yet has no meaning as such, at least as an adjective. His reading of lines from Yeats' poetic dramas in some room off Cromwell Road in West Kensington had the opposite effect – I just let the tears run.

I first saw Harold act in a production of Joe Brearley's in which he played Romeo. I don't know what year this was but it cannot have been much later than 1947; I could see that it was a powerful emotional performance, highly strung yet also very physical. Yet, he was not allowed to get away with complete uncritical adulation because of Moishe's side-of-mouth debunking. Later, in his front lounge room he'd read some lines from *Henry IV Part 2*, Act III – the conversation between Shallow and Silence which begins with Silence saying, 'We shall all follow, cousin' – to Shallow saying, 'And is old Double dead?' This occasion was a particularly powerful one. I felt a strong sense of kinship with him. I don't mean that we were both Jewish or anything like that. I mean that I felt I had from childhood a deep sense of my responsibility for my fellow humans and his reading of that passage at that time showed me he had a strong similar concern. Where has my concern got me, and what have I done with it?

So, Harold was, I knew then, someone rather special, a person who was self-directed and who knew (I speak from the future) that he had things to accomplish in the world of real people not in the world of shams. His very early piece called *Latest Reports from the Stock Exchange*, which I think I have somewhere, was a reaction to the hypocrisy and avarice in the world outside, that he must have felt so strongly while still at school. It began with a repetition of the headline from the London *Evening Standard* – 'Gottwald in Coma' and went on to give a commentary on the minute-by-minute changes in the prices of all kinds of shares, but done in racing/steeple-chasing terminology. It was a brilliant piece of writing. I think it is possible to see the enormous effect that such a personality can have on an impressionable boy at that time in Hackney.

I recall one very wrought moment for me when after just returning from Ireland for the first time, and having fallen in love there, he called in one evening after the rest of my family had gone to bed and began to read from the speech where Troilus doubts his ability to adequately love Cressida. I misinterpreted the intention of Harold to express the general feeling that all true lovers must feel about their own shortcomings in the light of the object of their own love. Instead, I felt that he was trying to instruct me in my own shortcomings, were I faced with a similar situation – which I was at that time with a Norwegian girl I had just become involved with. I felt strongly enough and hurt enough to ask him to leave, which of course he did; and I assume now that he would have been quite bewildered. My apologies to him took the form of a poetic likening of the loss of his friendship (through a complete misunderstanding on my part) to the sinking of a Spanish galleon filled with gold and emeralds.

We all were aware, I think, of the nature of Harold's great ability to share and empathise. Most people we come into contact with during our lives have, to a greater or lesser extent, to exhibit the qualities of a chameleon – changing their colour or spots to suit the times, or the occasion, for their own self-interest. It is my opinion that Harold is one of those too-uncommon individuals who has throughout, from the time I first got to know him, maintained an untarnished and consistent attitude to other people and to the life around him. There are not enough people around like that. I think Jimmy Law has this quality, and so did my late younger brother, David. I still think even now, how obvious it is that Pinter would be intolerant of falsity or meanness in anybody. In order for this to be so, there are certain things one has to sacrifice. But as he said recently, he can't be given the sack because he doesn't work for anyone. So he can afford to say what he likes. Take it or leave it.

Anyone lucky enough to know Harold or Jimmy as a friend must have a very high regard for them as supporting the kind of world we deserve and not necessarily the kind of world we have.

Well, well, to come to *The Dwarfs*. I think it is a very accurate picture of the mental or spiritual atmosphere we all breathed at that time. Things happened and they can't just be described in a chronological list. Such phrases as we uttered were true to the context in which they happened. Walking the streets – up and down – in Hackney, as thoughts came and went and some thoughts reached the air and were expressed, while most were chewed over in silence. More often it was the movement of the hips, of the summer breeze through a blouse, that spoke wordlessly and more meaningfully. Could it have been anywhere else but Hackney? In my view, Hackney was a decisive factor, in the kind of rarefied breakdown and rebuilding of a language that was foreign to Henry's and Moishe's parents and not that natural to mine either. That Hackney Downs School was a decisive factor in the nature and quality of its teaching staff and the natural acceptance by the non-Jews of its large and undoubtedly talented Jewish content. This is not to say that Pinter would not have become a force in literature even without these factors. I'm sure he would. But *The Homecoming* and *The Dwarfs* could hardly have been written. I just can't imagine his writing about the Number 136 (if there is such a bus) from Wimbledon to Purley. It just doesn't sound right.

I attended one of the first performances of Beckett's *Waiting for Godot* at the Arts Theatre in the late fifties at Harold's suggestion. Before this, Harold had already sent me extracts from Beckett's *Watt* from Ireland where he found them in *Irish New Writing*. We read *Murphy* (long out of print but buried in the stacks of the Westminster Public Library and placed on special request by Harold), *Malone Dies*, *Molloy*, *L'Innomable* and of course *Watt*. There was much to enthuse about. I found this writing something close to my own feeble attempts at facing the world through print. Kafka was another tremendous influence which Pinter introduced me to. There was a very close mutual recognition of the much larger world that remained unexpressed and often inexpressible behind the actual possibility of language as used in a day-to-day way. It was like discovering that the iceberg that we could see concealed a much bigger reality. I have to admit that I would often cajole him in my letters for not cultivating an explicitly 'moral' tone in his writing. I think he saw the bigger reality. At least he dismissed such a simplistic standpoint as mine – and quite rightly so.

I have kept all the letters Harold wrote to me from Ireland and since, of course. Before he left to join McMaster's company for the first time (I don't know the year), I saw him coming down the front steps of his house carrying quite a large bundle of papers. I just happened to be passing the house at 19 Thistlewaite Road on my way home to 5 Thornby Road. It was a pure coincidence. I asked what he was doing and he said he was clearing up a few old writings of his (which he intended to throw in the dustbin). I told him to give them to me and I would look after them for him. I kept these writings under my bed until he returned and then gave them back to him. It never occurred to me to delve into that pile of writing and read what he had done. I just gave them back to him. I imagine some of his early poems were amongst them. Of course, I read whatever Harold gave me of his early poems. I did not read them with the weight of being trained in an appreciation of English poesy resting on my shoulders. At that time I knew and appreciated little poetry. So perhaps I was lucky that I could read them uncritically, 'straight from the horse's mouth'. It was the sculptured richness of the language which I felt. The meaning lying thirty fathoms deep – inaccessible, but nevertheless, in some strange way, there. Some of the writing was, well, sparkling in its intensity, even if abstruse in its meaning. One could go on. I'm just trying to give you an idea what it was like to be part of the very first audience. It is something that I feel quite strongly about. When you know the person behind the poem, there is obviously a much warmer response. He did in fact dedicate his first volume of poetry to me, no doubt as a result of my rescuing his writings from the rubbish tip.

There is one facet of our many conversations which you might find interesting. I went to visit Harold in Northern Ireland where he was appearing in rep and I went over there for a short holiday. Jill Johnson was also acting in the same company at that time. It was in Portstewart, as we were walking along the cliffs with the sea not far off, that I mentioned to Harold the attempt by Janáček to capture speech rhythms and intonations of his native Czech in his music. Particularly in the string quartet 'Intimate Letters'. I wondered why no one had thought of doing the reverse. Of course it was a silly idea, but then it struck me that Beethoven used silence as a dramatic device in his symphonies. It was so powerful. His use of the rest in his music had an effect which Beethoven continued to use throughout his life. It was almost as if he'd invented it. No doubt other composers had used this device too before him, but none with such effect. I do not know whether this sunk in on Harold because it was well before he started writing plays, but in any case we all had some effect on each other in this way, by exploring our own thoughts out loud, and no one can claim to have had more effect than anyone else, or to have been completely original.

He seemed, in those early years, to be the first to sense the implications of new developments in film, the theatre, and in literature. So, you could say that in some ways he led and we followed; but it is not at all as cut and dried as that. I don't recollect any of us being a 'leader' as such. I mean, Henry discovered Gully Jimson in *The Horse's Mouth* by Joyce Carey and we all read that book. I felt very flattered at Harold's wanting to share his discovery of Beckett (and Kafka) with me. It may be that he had a similar urge to share other things with Henry, Moishe, Ron or Jimmy. I know I wanted to share my love of chamber music, of Schubert in particular, with him. I also mentioned at some point how impressed I was with L.P. Hartley's trilogy *Eustace and Hilda*. I loved his style of writing. Could this have been a factor in his doing *The Go-Between*? Harold has always had a passionate loyalty to his friends. At the same time he is just as passionately upset by any disloyalty. This comes over strongly in *The Dwarfs*. The public airing of a confidence is not to be tolerated. I hope I have not been guilty of that in this letter, and I hope that my remarks have been useful.

Henry Woolf

Article published in *The Guardian*, 14 January 2002.

It's been really inconvenient, Harold Pinter becoming famous like that. A great playwright, a cultural icon. If he hadn't, we might still be bowling about Hackney together, two lively old gents toddling off to the Sally Ann Sunset Home to be safely tucked up for the night. What with all his writing and acting and directing, I haven't seen half as much of him as I'd have liked over the years. Not to mention marriage, family and other friends – sizable interventions, you'll admit. And me? Well, yes – the world I thought to have stuffed securely up the fathomless recesses of my most trusted orifice suddenly turned nasty, and before I could say 'solipsist' I found myself married, with a family in tow, a working actor and, of all things, a professor. Cor! Up to my ears like everyone else in what is laughingly called life. Ah well.

I might have known the old order wasn't going to last when, by a bit of luck, I got the chance to direct the first production of Pinter's first play, *The Room*, way back in 1957, at the Bristol University Drama Department. On the first night the audience woke up from its polite cultural stupor and burst into unexpected life, laughing, listening, taking part in the story unfolding onstage. They had just been introduced to Pinterland, where no explanations are offered, no quarter given, and you have the best time in a theatre you've ever had in your life. After that, despite the efforts of some skilled theatrical assassins (you should read some of the reviews for

The Birthday Party from 1958 – pure poison), there was no stopping Pinter. He was away.

However, there are more insidious ways of nobbling a favourite than strangling him at birth – the grim hand of reverence, for instance. The first night of *The Room* in 1957 glittered with laughter and menace. (Good old Martin Esslin – what a wonderful phrase he coined: 'the comedy of menace'.) And the second production? Directed by some-one else. Pompous intimidation of the audience: 'No laughs please, this is art' – that sort of thing. The grim hand was already at work. It should never be underestimated. Look what it has already done to some wonderful playwrights – Chekhov, for example. Remember the awful, mummified productions, taken move for move from the original Stanis-lavsky prompt books, that the Moscow Arts Theatre used to bring to London? Dead as mutton. Great actors sleepwalk-ing through yesterday. Embalming fluid has been tried on Pinter often enough, but forty-five years after his first pro-duction he still comes up fresh as a daisy. He will never become a museum piece.

Over the next couple of weeks I will be performing Pinter's *Monologue* (at the National Theatre, no less – better than the end of the pier, eh?). It's an unbelievable treat. Pinter first asked me to do it in 1973 for the BBC. He could have had almost anyone play it. A world premiere of a Pinter play on national television – and a solo part to boot? Quite a few takers, one would think. But no, he asked me. Typically generous. Blindly loyal, some would say. He's the most loyal bloke I've ever met, especially to his old mates. He could have affectionately dumped us years ago, with no hard feelings and no visible bruises. But far from it – fifty years on we are all as close as ever, despite life's vicissitudes.

There are four of us left now. We used to bowl about Hackney in our late teens, kings of the world, constantly talking, constantly quoting plays, poems, stories. The world's demands took second place to our minds' imaginings. Pinter was ahead of us in just about everything. Way ahead with girls (a very sensitive area), but also in what he read and the films he saw. He educated us all, introduced us to Joyce, Beckett, Kafka, Dylan Thomas, took us to see movies by Buñuel and Dali. (I'll never forget the razor slashing the eyeball in *Un Chien Andalou*.) But did we show any signs of gratitude or respect? Not a bit of it. Pinter's explorations and adventures were often greeted with suspicion or dismay.

Pinter once 'borrowed' Beckett's novel *Murphy* from a Hoxton public library without a ticket. We rounded on him . . . 'What's that under your jacket? You've stolen a library book. Haven't you? Think of all the charladies who won't be able to read Beckett now.' Even when he pointed out that the book hadn't been taken out since 1939 (this was 1947), our indignation still frothed.

The truth was, he was a bit too much for us. And for some strange young man's reason, we would rather have died than show our affection and admiration for him.

Playing the Man in *Monologue* is like being on both sides of the mirror at once. The character's world of memory and regret is alive with echoes of the life we once shared as friends: 'You introduced me to Webster and Tourneur, admitted. But who got you going on Tristan Tzara, Breton, Giacometti, all that lot? Not to mention Louis-Ferdinand Céline, now out of favour, and John Dos? Who bought you all those custard tins cut-price?' Pinter introduced us to them all, of course. I don't know about the custard tins.

Monologue may share locations ('Balls Pond Road . . . the rain in the light on the pavements in the twilight') and situations ('the sweet, the sweet, the sweet farewell of Paddington

Station . . . nothing like the sound of steam to keep love warm, to keep it moist, to bring it to the throat') with the real world, the bygone world, but the play itself is something quite other – an extended dramatic poem, very funny and very sad. It is a little masterpiece written by someone at the top of his form. Each time I play *Monologue* I hear echoes of other times and other places, but they come from far away. I'm on the other side of the mirror now, alone in a vivid landscape, wandering in Pinterland.

Actors and Directors

Peter Hall

Peter Hall interviewed by Catherine Itzin and
Simon Trussler in *Theatre Quarterly*, No. 16, 1974.

*Sir Peter Hall is without doubt one of Pinter's great collaborators
and interpreters. During the 1960s and 1970s his work helped
consolidate Pinter's reputation and set the tone for performances
of the work. His comments in this interview on rehearsal and on
detailed approaches to language are invaluable. In retrospect,
some of Hall's assumptions and comments raise questions.
Was he right in thinking that the true and proper destiny of
Pinter's work was to 'free itself' entirely from its roots in 'rep'
plays? Was Hall right in seeing Pinter almost entirely in terms
of a high cultural canon (in the interview he invokes Mozart,
Kafka, Beckett and others) when other directors have profitably
explored the comic and popular elements of Pinter? Certainly
Hall speaks confidently of what he sees as the limitations of
audiences in a way that few other contributors to this volume do.*

*One of the less expected results of Peter Hall's momentous years
as Artistic Director of the Royal Shakespeare Company was the
close association he developed with the work of Harold Pinter.
Pinter himself, notorious for his reluctance to talk about his own
plays, worked alongside Hall to create what were (at least for
their times) definitive productions of* The Homecoming *(1965),*
Landscape *(1969),* Silence *(1969), and* Old Times *(1971) – not
to mention the adaptation of* The Collection *from television to
stage, which first sparked the relationship in 1962. In this
interview with Catherine Itzin and Simon Trussler, Peter Hall
discusses for the first time in detail his own approach to directing*

Pinter, and the problems and rewards the plays have for actors and director alike.

★

You're now the director one associates most closely with Pinter, but actually the association began relatively late in his career, didn't it?

In practice, yes. But Pinter had seen my production of *Godot* back in 1956 or 1957, and [the producer] Michael Codron sent me *The Birthday Party* when it was first going to be done. I didn't know who Harold Pinter was, but I liked the play enormously. I couldn't do it though, because I had commitments in New York that year: and when *The Caretaker* was sent to me, I couldn't do that, either . . . But I did put £250 into the production of *The Caretaker* at the Arts, which I think was capitalised at £1000 or something very low, and it earned me a surprising amount of money – it's one of the few times I've made money out of investing in plays . . . I then put most of the money back into the film of *The Caretaker*.

Can you remember now how you reacted when you first read The Birthday Party *by this unknown dramatist?*

Well, I heard the voice of Beckett, without any question, and the voice of Kafka – the horror, the terror of the unknown. But I did think the play was rather too bound by its own naturalism: you know, the three-act structure, the French's Acting Edition set. That was why I was so thrilled when I read *The Caretaker*, which seemed to have reached a point where the form was uniquely the dramatist's own. I don't think *The Birthday Party* is quite free from being a 'rep' play.

You didn't consider The Caretaker *for the opening Aldwych season?*

[132]

Oh no, I couldn't. Michael Codron had an option on *The Caretaker*, having done *The Birthday Party* and lost his shirt on that.

Donald McWhinnie directed the premiere. How well did you like his production?

I certainly liked it well enough to ask him to do, I think, three productions with the RSC. I didn't think it was quite hard enough, actually. It was a little explanatory – perhaps Pinter needed to be at that stage.

By the time you eventually co-directed The Collection *with Pinter for the RSC, he had written quite a few other radio and television plays – why choose to stage* The Collection *in particular?*

He hadn't got a new play ready at that time, and we were trying to find something from among the other pieces which would be viable on stage. We decided to do it together for a number of reasons. I think it's true that Harold actually wanted to learn to be a director, and thought that collaboration would be a sensible way to begin.

And how did you respond to The Collection?

Well, working on Pinter's plays over the years, I'm conscious, retrospectively, of having developed a technique, an approach, a way of going about things. I certainly didn't have that when we began *The Collection*. But it was very much part of the same world as working on Beckett – making the actor trust what is given, making him accept the premise of the words. That goes as much for the architectural shape of the words as it does for any resonance that they may have for the actor emotionally. And since you cannot actually ignore or change the words, you may as well start from there. The parallel to me is with music – don't get me wrong, I don't think if you merely sing the right notes, you make any sense in human terms. You don't in opera, you don't in Pinter. But if you sing the *wrong* notes you are going to make nonsense. And certainly, even in *The Collection*, there was a great discipline required of the actor, to trust the text.

It's always seemed to me one of Pinter's more paradoxical plays, in that it's all about the search for verification, trying to pin things down, yet there can't really be a 'right' answer as far as the audience is concerned ...

Well, I think you have to take an attitude yourself about what happens. You may decide that the audience should not be let in on the total secret. *Old Times* belongs to the same world. What is truth? What is memory? What actually happened?

But you think it is possible, at least for the purposes of the actors, to say what actually happened?

Oh yes. You must. Or what happened for one particular actor. It may be different from one actor to another. Certainly, for the audience, part of the problem was to keep the enigma intact – I mean, of what actually happened in Leeds in *The Collection*. All you can do for the actors is to discover what needs to have happened in Leeds for each of them, so that their behaviour will make human and emotional sense. And if you ask Pinter what happened in Leeds, he does say, 'What needs to have happened in Leeds? What does it say?' Well, that's fair enough, I think. Pinter productions which remove the ambiguous, the contradictory, the enigmatic, actually become very simplistic and boring. The image lacks complexity, and is then *unlike* memory, because it is uncontradictory.

On the other hand, don't you think that if you have a play like The Collection, *in which there is an objective truth out there somewhere to be found, and the characters are searching for it, isn't there an inevitable danger of removing the enigma for the audience? That they will get so concerned about what 'really' happened that they lose track of what seems to me the most interesting aspect of* The Collection, *which is the shifting inter-relationships between the characters?*

Yes, I agree. I'm not really very qualified to talk about *The Collection* at this distance of time. I no longer know it very well. But the same gradual unfolding of problems goes on in all the other plays. Teddy's marriage in *The Homecoming* . . . where does that girl come from? Does she really come from quite near the house? What actually happened in *Old Times* – I mean, who was in love with whom? I think it's no accident that Pinter is fascinated by Proust, and the shift of memory – the fact that your reporting of this conversation will be totally different from mine, and yet we're both accurate within our own obsessions.

At the same time, Old Times *is about old times, and there is a dramatic context for the memory to play tricks, whereas* The Collection *is about something that happened, what, some two or three weeks ago . . .*

But yesterday is long enough ago for the memory to play tricks . . . Yet it's a fair point. I do think that the early Pinter is much more enigmatic than later Pinter, and can irritate. I mean, exactly what are Goldberg and McCann up to? What organisation do they work for?

He traded, I think, on ominous vagueness at times, in the early work. His advance as a dramatist is that he's become more and more concrete, making plays depend on the strong dramatic conflicts which underlie *The Homecoming*, or *Old Times*, or even *Landscape*. At first sight it is an enigma, but the situation, if you attend to the play, is blindingly clear.

Can you describe the process of work on The Collection?

I am the final arbiter of the production, and he, obviously, is the final arbiter of the text. I think this has, on occasion, been very tough on the actors, because we do develop a kind of Tweedledum and Tweedledee act, and we are, I think, very good for each other. But that doesn't necessarily mean we're very good for some of the actors surrounding us. It's all a bit high-powered, it's very wordy, and we split hairs with great glee. The scrutiny can get a bit much. But Harold will never say, 'You shouldn't do *that*.' He will say, 'That isn't right,' which is something quite different.

Is there an example of that you could give?

Well, let's take *The Homecoming*. The problem there is that the biggest bastard in a house full of bastards is actually the man who at first sight appears to be the victim – that is, Teddy, the brother who brings his wife home. He is actually locked in a battle of wills with his father and with his brothers, and of course, with his wife, during which, in some sense, he destroys his wife, and his family, and his father, and himself, rather than give in. He is actually the protagonist. Now, it's very easy for an actor to fall into the 'martyred' role in that part, because Teddy says so little – just sits there while all the other characters are speculating about his wife's qualities in bed. But this is the point – it's a tremendous act of will on his part to take it, and if he was actually feeling anything uncontrolled, he wouldn't be able to do it.

It wasn't until Michael Jayston did it in the film that I realised how hard Teddy actually had to be, and how much in control he was. I'd felt it, but I hadn't pushed it far enough. And Harold was always saying to me, during the two stage productions, 'That's not quite right.'

★

My approach to a Pinter play is first of all to try and expose the underlying melodrama of the text. I try and find out who does hate who, and who loves who, and who's doing what to whom, and in the first stage of rehearsals play it very crudely.

Does this mean that you try to find what is actually happening, in fact, so far as there might be a fact?

Yes. There is a fact. Certainly there is a fact. Why, in *The Homecoming*, is Lenny so obsessed from the word go with destroying his father? Talking about his cooking and his rotten meals and so on. Now that must not, in my view, be played with any kind of heaviness: but the underlying feeling is one of absolute naked hatred. Because I think at the base of a good deal of Harold's work is the cockney game of taking the piss: and part of that game is that you should not be quite sure whether the piss is being taken or not. In fact, if you know I'm taking the piss, I'm not really doing it very well: and a good deal of Harold's tone has to do with that very veiled kind of mockery.

Now, actors can't play veiling until they know what they're veiling, so we play mockery, we play hatred, we play animosity, we play the extreme black-and-white terms of a character. That stage of rehearsal is very crude, but it's a very important stage, because unless the actor understands what game he is playing, what his actual underlying motivations are, the ambiguity of the text will mean nothing. People who think that all you've got to do in Pinter is to say it, hold the pause, and then say the next line, are wrong. The mystery to me is that there is a communication in the theatre which is beyond words, and which is actually concerned with direct feeling. An actor who says to you, 'All right, I may be feeling that, but unless I show the audience that I'm feeling it, they won't understand,' is actually wrong. If he feels it and masks it, the audience still gets it.

Would it be possible to illustrate that in terms, say, of how Harry and Bill related to each other in the early rehearsals of The Collection?

Well, that marvellous 'slum-slug' speech, *that's* taking the cockney piss, absolutely. He is masking his hatred and self-disgust by the level of the mockery he is expressing, but he has to have it inside. So I think the crude melodrama is very important to find and discover. Harold usually stays away from those rehearsals.

Do you find the actors have very definite feelings initially, even if they're wrong ones, rather than just feeling confused?

It very much depends on the actor. You see, because he has such a distinctive voice, very quickly there came to be a 'Pinter style,' which is external. Actors know you speak Pinter in a dry, clipped way, and you hold the pause, and you don't inflect very much, and you don't show very much emotion. It's wrong, of course – a convention, nothing more. Like saying play Chekhov sad, or Shakespeare with a lot of lung power. But, very early on, one felt actors making Pinter patterns, and that's really dreadful, though I suppose it's better than actors trying to 'normalise' Pinter's speech rhythms, because the first thing I say to actors when we're beginning a Pinter play is 'Look, don't mislead yourselves into thinking that if there's a pause there, or, if there's a silence, there shouldn't be a silence, because there should. Our job is to find out why. And don't, in order to make it comfortable, turn a full stop into a comma, or break it up in a colloquial way different to the way he's written it.'

I actually believe that Beckett and Pinter are poetic dramatists, in the proper sense of the word: they have a linear structure and a formal structure which you'd better just observe – don't learn it wrong, don't speak it wrong, you can't, you mustn't. But there are various things that you can exercise. One of the greatest influences on Pinter, obviously, is the early Eliot – particularly in the repeated phrase, the catching up of a phrase and repeating it over three sentences, keeping it up in the air, like a ball. Now, that is often written in three separate sentences: but it has to make a unit, and you don't find that unit till about the third week. So at the beginning it is better just to observe absolutely accurately what he's written.

I also know that the intensity of the feeling underlying Pinter's text is so very extreme, so very brutal, that you have to explore this melodramatic area that I was speaking about.

My vocabulary is all the time about hostility and battles and weaponry, but that is the way Pinter's characters operate, as if they were all stalking round a jungle, trying to kill each other, but trying to disguise from one another the fact that they are bent on murder. And whether you can see a character's face or whether you can't, whether you hold his eyes or not, is absolutely critical – and that, to a very large extent, comes out of the actor's psyche, once the feelings are being generated. So I wouldn't have anything to say about the physical life of a Pinter play until the emotions had been released, because I wouldn't know what they should be. Equally, Pinter deals in stillness, in confrontations which are unbroken, and I believe it mandatory to do as few moves in a Pinter play as possible. You don't want moves up to the drinks cabinet, or across the table, in order to 'break it up,' or to make it seem naturalistic. It isn't naturalistic.

I couldn't help feeling that John Bury's cavernous set for the Aldwych production of The Homecoming *almost cried out for the actors to make just those sorts of irrelevant moves . . .*

But they didn't.

No, but to some extent the set seemed to work against what you've just said.

[139]

No, I don't think that's true at all. Pinter wrote *The Home-coming* for the Aldwych, actually. His description of the set is that it is enormous, and actually the staircase was twice as tall as an actual staircase would have been. The area they were fighting over, which was the father's chair and the sofa where the seduction takes place, and the rug in front, was an island in the middle of antiseptic cleanliness – that scrubbed lino, acres of it. And the journey from that island where the family fought each other, across to the sideboard to get the apple, was very perilous, and this was all quite deliberate – a few objects in space, and a feeling of absolute chilliness and hostility.

Pinter has got a terrific selectivity about physical life on the stage. His stage directions, if he needs to give them, about where people move and what they do, are extremely precise, and if he doesn't give them, it's just as well to assume that nothing is necessary. This also goes for design. If the set for *The Homecoming* is a naturalistic representation of a house in North London, then the glass of water makes almost no impression, because it's one glass among many knick-knacks. I think one of the troubles about *The Birthday Party* as a play was that Pinter hadn't yet achieved in formal terms, the absolute clarity of his vision. *The Birthday Party* exists in that rather cluttered room, it's all more unnecessarily naturalistic.

I'd agree about The Birthday Party, *but the clutter seems absolutely vital to* The Caretaker.

Oh yes, it is. But that is a *decision* to be very cluttered, and that's a point in itself. Equally, *The Homecoming* is about space, and I think *Old Times* is about those two beds side by side. And sometimes they're sofas. Pinter has an immensely architectural sense.

You've mentioned cockney piss-taking as a recurrent element in Pinter's plays. Are there other important features they share?

If anybody breaks down in a Pinter play, it is catatonic . . . total. A breakdown is a sign of great, great weakness – the end of the world. So most of the characters preserve their cool, however hot their cool is inside. Equally, physical violence can suddenly be unleashed, which is an expression of the tensions that have been developing beneath this often very urbane surface, and people crack each other over the head or beat each other up or kill each other. It's there in that sudden unleashing, that total breakdown of Deeley at the end of *Old Times*.

Don't you think there's any difference in this respect between the two worlds in which Pinter's plays seem to be set – one of them the North London or the cockney world, the other the much more urbane, middle-class world, from The Collection *onwards?*

I don't think there is very much difference. There are different kinds of sophistications, but his cockney characters are extremely clever, extremely sophisticated. But the other recurring characteristic concerns his treatment of women. It is very sensitive and well-observed – he creates wonderful women; but always one feels it's a *man* looking at women, the feminine enigma remains.

But isn't there a difference here between the younger and the older women? The older women seem to be observed more from the inside – the older women from Landscape *and* Silence, *for example.*

Yes, I think you're right. He has a more romantic approach to them, a greater compassion and understanding. I think Beth is an astonishing creation of regrets – very feminine, very romantic. But the women in his plays who remain sex objects – sexually active, attractive to men – are all enigmatic, and dangerous, in some sense.

Do you find improvisation is of any value in trying to get at the nature of the underlying tensions?

You can't improvise easily as an aid to acting Pinter, because at the end of the day you still have to speak a very formal text. But you can improvise feeling patterns, or you can play the opposites – say, 'Let's play this scene with you hating instead of loving.' Or you can increase the obvious underlying tensions, you can swap roles – you can do all the things that make people aware of the underlying tensions. To that extent improvisation is helpful . . . the second stage is to find how to disguise the emotions which are quite evidently being felt. When Ruth returns with Teddy and comes downstairs in the morning and the father is so dreadful to her and to his son, 'having tarts in the house at night,' the obvious realistic response would be to break down left and bury your head in the sofa, or whatever. But he beckons her over to him, the father does, and she crosses and looks him in the eye, and he says to her, 'How many kids have you got?' 'Three.' 'All yours, Ted?' Now, by any normal standards of improvisation, Ruth should be playing that scene hysterically, but she isn't. The alarm is underneath, but totally masked.

And the actress knows why she isn't hysterical?

Oh, of course. Because she's taking the old man on. If the old man is making that kind of challenge, she is accepting it. It doesn't mean to say she's not upset, underneath her mask, just as in the last section of the play, when Teddy is deliberately pushing the family, they retaliate with the proposition that his wife should be put on the game, as a dreadful joke at first, to see if he'll crack. And he is saying throughout the last twenty minutes of the play, 'You live your joke. Go on. You want to put her on the game? You needn't think I'll object. *Put* her on the game.' He's dying inside, because he doesn't, of course, want to lose his wife. But again, the mask is not allowed to slip. There's one little crack at the end of the play, the most difficult moment of the play, when he's leaving the room, and Ruth says, 'Don't become a stranger.' It is very difficult to play. That's the first and only time she calls him Eddie, which is obviously the intimate and familiar name. It is all there, and it is all very . . . calculated is the wrong word, because I know Harold to be a deeply instinctive writer, who writes very quickly once it's there to be written, and it would not be true to say that he works it all out like an intellectual game.

It's almost as if you have to direct two plays each time you direct a Pinter play . . . ?

Yes, you do, you certainly do. And I think the achievement of a Pinter production must be that the two plays meet. Because what stirs the audience is not the mask, not the control, but what is underneath it.

Are you partly saying that there are really no weak characters in Pinter's plays – weak in the human sense? Ready to give in and to react naturally.

No, I don't think so. Uncle Sam is very weak, but he's also very sly and very cunning, because he knows the dangers of the game. That's why, when he makes the final revelation in *The Homecoming*, that 'McGregor had Jessie in the back of my cab as I drove them along,' there's nothing for him to do but keel over, pass out, the pressure is so much. I do think that Harold has recognised from the beginning of his writing that if, say, I'm sitting in this room on my own, I'm in a totally relaxed state – I don't know how my face is behaving, I'm not concerned about it, I'm not presenting myself to anybody. A knock on the door, by you, is sufficient to make my face form a pattern, even before you've actually entered, and from that moment on, neither of us, either by word or by deed or in physical relation to each other, are expressing what we are actually feeling. We are modifying ourselves in relation to each other . . . We are playing the game – that is, social intercourse.

Once the play is beginning to live, you cannot be too meticulous. What Pinter wrote is always better than what a lazy actor will come up with. Now, this may seem a very small and pedantic point, but most of our actors have a fairly easy-going, not to say contemptuous, attitude to what a dramatist has written, and for the average playwright, writing the average colloquial flim-flam, it doesn't matter very much whether you say 'but' instead of 'and', or put in a few extra words. It does in Pinter, and it is excruciatingly difficult to get it completely accurate. But *when* you get it accurate, then the rhythm – and he has the most astonishing ability to write rhythms – begins to work. And you begin to feel the emotions underlying those rhythms. Let me put it like this. If you sing a Mozart aria correctly, certain responses begin to be necessary inside you. Now, you could say that's putting the cart before the horse, but that's the way it is – you're not improvising something of your own, you're singing some notes of Mozart. It's much the same with Pinter.

You can do that too early, and then you simply have the actor imitating surface rules. He must already be alive in himself, emotionally, otherwise it's an imposition.

There is a difference in Pinter between a pause and a silence and three dots. A pause is really a bridge where the audience think that you're this side of the river, then when you speak again, you're the other side. That's a pause. And it's alarming, often. It's a gap, which retrospectively gets filled in. It's not a dead stop – that's a silence, where the confrontation has become so extreme, there is nothing to be said until either the temperature has gone down, or the temperature has gone up, and then something quite new happens. Three dots is a very tiny hesitation, but it's there, and it's different from a semi-colon, which Pinter almost never uses, and it's different from a comma. A comma is something that you catch up on, you go through it. And a full stop's just a full stop. You stop.

Have you found that, because of the clichés that have developed about Pinter, actors try to leap over your first few weeks of rehearsal, and go straight into the significance bit?

Yes, and that's disastrous, that's disastrous.

At what point would Pinter himself normally have started to come along and tell you if things weren't right?

From the word go. He pops in every few days. The great thing about Pinter is that he knows what work processes are, he's not one of those dramatists who judges today's work as if it were the first night. He's a practical man of the theatre.

[After the strong emotion for each character has been established] is a very difficult stage of rehearsal, because often actors feel that they are going to have to throw away those feelings, which they have so carefully nurtured, if they're going to be that evident, and that criticised, they're going to throw them away altogether, and start feeling like hollow shells with a mask on top. So it's all a matter of balance, of going from one extreme, then back to the other again. After that stage, I have a very technical, shaping period of rehearsal which is equally horrible, because, I shape what's been found – that is, I make certain quick bits quicker, slow up some slow bits, find motives to make this pause longer or that pause shorter. I do a whole rehearsal of the play in which the main thing is to see how quickly you can take the cues, if there isn't a pause or silence. I orchestrate it, actually. But only from what has been reached. Shape what has been found.

I think a Pinter play usually needs about five or six weeks. One of the reasons why it needs a long time is that a concentrated Pinter rehearsal is so exhausting for actors they can't take more than about four hours a day without actually cheating for the fifth or sixth, or just getting so taut that it doesn't work. Four to five hours a day is about the maximum they can take.

The ideal way to work on a Pinter play would be to rehearse it for three weeks, and then design the set. Of course, we're never in that situation. I've only been able to do that once in my life, and that was for an Albee production. When it comes to sets, costumes, props, I think everything burns itself so strongly on the audience's mind in a Pinter play that the coffee cup really has to be very carefully considered. It sounds very fanciful, but the apples in *The Homecoming* had to be green – they could not be yellow or red, because they simply didn't disturb visually. The moment when Sam picks up the apple and eats it and says, 'Feeling a bit peckish' to the old man, is a kick in the crutch to him, and a soft yellow apple would not have had the same effect, I sound obsessive, I am. The furniture, the costumes, are very, very carefully scrutinised and a lot of things change, until one builds up something where one can feel that each second is charged with something, and is right.

The artist that I have thought about visually for Pinter, ever since I read *The Birthday Party*, is Magritte – that hard-edged, very elegant, very precise style. Again, you see, you can't overstate. I remember in *Old Times* initially Vivien Merchant's Anna had a very elegant, rather warm reddish dress. It *wasn't* red, it was reddish, but it made a total statement of the Scarlet Woman as soon as she walked on to the stage, and it had to change for that reason.

I remember having the impression of her being slightly old-fashioned, somehow.

That's correct, that was deliberate. She wore blue suede, in the end. Memory, and all that – for that first image of her standing there during the first scene, when you don't know whether she's actually there or what.

To what extent did you figure out whether she was there or not?

Well, she's not there, in actual, naturalistic terms, but she is there, because she's been there for twenty years, in each of their heads. She's never left either of their heads, and she never will. She can't leave the room at the end. She tries to, it is impossible. Actually, the two of them would not stay married, they wouldn't stay related, they wouldn't almost exist, without the obsession of that third person in their heads, and the opening image illustrates that. It's a reaching towards a kind of imagery – an emblem in silence. The exciting thing about Harold is that I'm fairly certain that areas of what one can loosely call physical symbolism are probably what he's going to get concerned with in the future.

Vivien Merchant has acted in many of Pinter's plays, and being his wife, obviously is very intimate with the world of the plays. I would have thought there were potential problems as well as advantages in that . . . possibly in knowing too much at the beginning . . .

The fact is that as an actress, she has this amazing precision, yet her enigmatic quality is quite genuine. She is absolutely in the centre of what Pinter's theatre is about, what a Pinter actor ought to be. And not least because she trusts her instincts absolutely, when she's doing his stuff, yet disguises what the instincts are producing. She's not one for sitting around having long chats about motivation or this or that or the other, she accepts what she's given, and tries to find a reality to support it.

Instinctively?

Instinctively. And, you know . . . I must emphasise that most of what I am talking about is making shapes out of instincts. Because I direct totally instinctively, and the only misery I know as a director is when I'm saying to myself, 'What

ought I to do?' When that question needs to be asked, you're
directing badly.

*How much more or less vital is the whole preliminary casting
process in a Pinter play?*

Well, I think the one thing you've got to do in casting a
Pinter play is cast rich personalities, because his characters
are like three-dimensional masks – we look at them from
different sides and we see different aspects of them, and
they've got to be fascinating people, in the first instance. So
I wouldn't cast good, dull actors. They have got to have
enormous verbal dexterity, and enormously good breath
control, because Pinter doesn't allow you to take ordinary
breaths, you know. You can't colloquialise it. Experience in
Shakespeare is a help.

*Yet one of the seeming things about a Pinter text is its apparent
linguistic simplicity . . .*

That really is only apparent. You take a piece of Pinter and
read it aloud as if you were in a TV Wednesday Play, and
you'll find that the emphases come at the wrong moments,
because you've run out of breath, and you can't quite get
your tongue around it, it doesn't quite work . . . My experience has been that the actor with a fair amount of classical
training and experience can handle it, but the actor who is
used to colloquial behaviourism can't do it at all.

*Getting back to the progress of rehearsals – have we got to the
stage where it's 'fixed,' but very difficult to hold?*

We're at the nit-picking stage. I've shaped it and orchest-
rated it, and it goes absolutely dead, and at this point you
have to do some exercises about what's actually being felt all
over again. You may even take the mask off in a couple of
scenes, in order to revitalise the emotional levels. I've done
that before now.

Does anybody panic?

Well, yes, people panic. I remember one very eminent actress panicking very badly at that stage, because she was being
confronted with an intensity of emotional life which she
didn't actually want to admit, certainly not on the stage,
and certainly not in life. But she played it, she played a
whole scene with tears running down her face, in actual
agony, and the other actors wanted to stop it but didn't dare,
because there was such a release going on. That is a measure
of the intensity of feeling required. Once she'd got that,
once we'd gone through that, it was all right.

So, at this stage I would say one is nit-picking about precise
timings, precise inflections, precise patterns, precise orches-
trations, which is all formalised and deadening. And at the
other extreme, one is stoking up the fires of feeling all the
time, so it's a crisis-ridden time. The other important point
is that an actor's responsibility to his fellows in Pinter is
absolutely critical. If an actor gives too much away or too
little on a feed-line, it makes it absolutely impossible to play
the answering line. So the actors must have developed – by
now we're in the fifth week – a trust and an understanding
of each other. At this point one is running the play probably
once a day, or certainly once every two days, and doing
exercises to make it more emotional on the one hand, and
shaping it technically on the other.

And then the most difficult thing of all comes when you
meet the audience, because a Pinter actor has to control the
audience in a quite deliberate way. It requires a degree of
control in the actor, a degree of arrogance in the actor,
towards the audience. For instance, you need to let an audience laugh in Pinter, so that at the precise moment when
they have laughed themselves out, you can hit them hard
with the actuality. The plays are constructed like that, and it
has to do with that tenth part of the actor's mind, which has

got nothing to do with truth, but with control and technique – the tenth of you standing outside and watching the whole thing. You have to be absolutely adroit.

You've described the creation of a very precisely-honed instrument, which is the finished production . . . how do you reconcile the precision of the thing on the one had, and the erraticism of the audience on the other?

Audiences are not that erratic for Pinter, actually. I think the precision is the instrument of control, and you can slightly increase the pause, or slightly increase the length of a laugh in order to grip a particular audience. Pinter audiences get off the hook and laugh at people as objects if you don't control them. You really have to make them listen, you really do have to hear that pin drop, and that takes a degree of expertise in the actor which is, I think, pretty considerable. But all the time, the paradox remains, about this intensity of feeling. That has to be utterly true. Because I have seen my own productions of Pinter, without the actors being aware of it, dry out in a fortnight or three weeks, so that the level of intensity underlying the masks has dropped, and actually what is being seen is a very chic series of patterns.

I was going to ask about this difficulty of having tuned a production to this pitch of intensity, and then having to keep it playing in the repertoire for months or even years.

You've got to keep attending to the emotional life underlying the play. That's the main thing.

Though Pinter himself now has a lot of experience as a director, he seems to have stopped directing his own plays . . .

Well, we tried this. I persuaded him to do the Aldwych revival of *The Birthday Party* himself . . . But the curious thing about *The Birthday Party* when he directed it was that the actors were not working in a free and open way with the director, they were working with the *author*. So when Harold said, and I heard him say it, 'I don't know, what does it say?' or 'Why don't you try . . . ?' they took it as God's writ. Therefore they acted results and simplifications. They didn't go on a quest. They didn't make something complex, which changed from second to second. This is the pain and the fascination of playing Pinter. You have this storm of emotion inside you, and you change tack, as we do in life, from second to second, behind the mask. This didn't happen in *The Birthday Party* production, because however Harold reacted, whether he said nothing or whether he said something, they took it to be *the answer*, and he said to me after he'd done that, 'I'm not going to direct any of my plays again. Not my plays. That's it.' Because it really didn't work.

On the whole you've tended to talk about Pinter's work as if it were a unified entity – do the production problems actually not vary a lot from one play to another?

I've been talking very much about *The Homecoming*, actually, which I personally regard as his greatest and biggest play. I think that what happened in *Landscape* and *Silence* was a very exciting herald for the future, which hasn't yet quite developed, although I think the Proust film-script he's recently done is well on the way. We've spoken a lot about hostility and jungle warfare and all the rest, but the other fascination, the other obsession in Pinter's world is trying to pin down reality, trying to pin down memory, trying to pin down truth: which is why Proust is so important to him, and why he's managed to reduce those twelve novels to 212 pages of images, which actually do work. It's the most extraordinary thing to read. And *Silence*, particularly, was a beautiful, heartbreaking evocation of the contradictions of memory. I would think that the problems of what is true, what is false, are going to go on being an obsession with him.

That particular theme was much more explicit in Old Times, *was it not?*

Much more literally explicit, yes.

I think it was because of the literalness that I didn't like it as well as Landscape *and* Silence. *In those plays it almost doesn't matter at any stage whose version of reality is valid.*

No, but I think what is remarkable about *Old Times* is that Deeley's own sexual insecurities, personal inadequacies, actually make him invent relationships and happenings which were not, in my view, true at all. The play is not about two lesbians, in spite of Visconti [who directed the Italian stage premiere]. They are not lesbian.

Perhaps the more important in that we don't seem to have mentioned design a great deal . . . ?

Exactly. That's why I'm mentioning John Bury now. And also, he is not a chatterer. He makes. He doesn't talk.

You mean you don't have long sessions with him, discussing how the set's going to be?

No. I give him an image. And we work from facts. From objects or models. I remember I had a piece of mirror, mirror tile actually, from somewhere in my house, and I just put it up at an angle on the stage: and that was the *Silence* set. John made the set with the split in it for *Landscape* without any comment at all. We communicate with grunts and objects, really, not with theories. I really believe that in the theatre – though you might not think it after all this chatter – you shouldn't talk, you should do, and you should look at what you've done rather than talk about what you might do.

In *The Homecoming*, Harold envisaged that vast room. 'We knocked the wall down several years ago to make an open living area. My mother was dead.' Because of the big Aldwych stage, John's first solution had a big iron beam across where they'd knocked the wall down. The iron was very evident, and I remember Harold saying, 'Now I think they would have put that big steel beam up, to keep the house up, that's right, and I like the whole proportion of it, but I don't want to see all that iron, that makes too much of a statement.' So we covered it with plaster. So you thought, well, maybe it's a big iron beam they've got there, but you weren't absolutely sure. That's an image, actually, of the whole process – the iron beam is there, but covered over.

Still, coming back to *Landscape,* I think the amazing thing about *Landscape,* and *Silence,* too, for that matter, is that staccato contests between two characters scoring off each other have given way to very involved, long prose passages which are organic – where one sentence depends on another, which have an emotional life, and which one actor can sustain. It's sustained poetic writing.

And you now get the staccato effect by the juxtaposition, as opposed to the direct interaction?

That's right. By the apparently random cross-cuts. Although we found in *Landscape* that one or two of the memories triggered off in Beth, for the actor anyway, seemed to come from the half-apprehension of what she'd heard Duff say. I made a film of it at the end of last year, which was very interesting, because a good deal of Beth is voice-over, with the face still, and it works very oddly. And for the extended passages she's in another place – there's nothing, you get a vague whiteness behind her, but she's talking. Then she's back again in the kitchen, her face still.

My feeling is that they need to be there together, with just the split down the stage. They're so interdependent . . .

You thought the split was too . . .

No, no, the split is fine onstage, because you can see the two characters there, but I can't envisage it working with them utterly separated.

Well, it was a difficult film to make, simply because she couldn't be talking in that room. There had to be a cinematic equivalent of the split.

That's the great advantage of the theatre.

Exactly. I mean, in the theatre we believe what we're told to believe. In a film we only believe what we see, and if we see a lady sitting in a room talking, then the other fellow hears her, doesn't he? It's very curious.

On the other hand, the plays which have been written originally for radio and television have been adapted very successfully to the stage – or rather, haven't had to be adapted to the stage. Exactly the same text is used, as with The Collection, *and it just works, with only one or two exceptions, in the theatre.*

I think the same thing goes with translating the plays to film: they just *work*, and it's actually because the voice – what is written, what the characters actually say – is so particular, and so absolutely clear, that it can move from one medium to another.

In spite of the general rule that things don't adapt, at least easily, from one medium to another?

I think it is because the voice of the writer is so particular, so absolute, that you don't talk about a play, or a film, or a radio or television play: you talk about Pinter, and Pinter's world. Certainly, there is very little difference between the experience of *The Homecoming* on the stage and *The Homecoming* on film – in fact, I think that on film it's slightly more disturbing, because the intensity is slightly greater.

But we didn't have to do anything to the dialogue. It cut so rhythmically and so strongly – that is, there are blocks of dialogue which have different intentions, and therefore different tempos, different atmospheres, and they break down into shots with almost no change. It's no accident that Pinter is a first-rate screen writer. That isn't because he's deliberately doing screen-writing – it just happens that the way he writes, the way he constructs dialogue, fits very naturally into a number of camera set-ups.

I suppose that the other development I sensed in Landscape *and* Silence *was that whereas previously people were antagonistic towards each other, in conflict with one another, here were a couple and a trio whose lives almost couldn't have been lived without one another . . .*

Dependence on each other . . . yes, I think that's true. But equally I think one could make a case that in *The Caretaker* and *The Homecoming* the hostility *is* the dependence. You must remember Pinter's Portuguese blood, I think. There is a kind of correctness, a pride, and a readiness for anger – in his writing, that is, I'm not speaking of him as a person!

And how important do you think the Jewishness is?

Very, in some areas – the extremity of family affection – the family unit being something which holds and encloses and makes everything possible, and yet also destroys everything. I don't say that is something which is special to the Jewish race, but it's something which they seem to have an extreme instinct for. But we all do it. Again, though, they are not 'Jewish' plays; to say that *The Homecoming* is about a Jewish family is already wrong. It isn't. And we went out of our way to make sure that they were not 'Jewish' actors.

We've talked about Beckett, and one can see the Beckettian associations, of course. But, whereas one feels that Beckett's characters are always hovering on the edge of some extremity of existence, in however comic a fashion, Pinter's world is much more part of one's own experience . . . almost, more normal.

I think that Pinter is concerned with the family unit, the husband-wife relationship, the child – the hope of making the bourgeois unit: whereas Sam's work is entirely concerned with 'me alone in a dark tunnel' – or you alone in a dark tunnel.

The difference perhaps between Willie and Winnie in Happy Days *and Beth and Duff in* Landscape. *There they are rubbing along together, although they're not actually apparently talking to each other . . .*

Exactly. I think that's a fair comment.

We've talked about the influences upon Pinter – of Beckett, and of Proust. Do you think that his influence on other playwrights has been fruitful or otherwise?

Well, I don't think you can blame anybody for the influence that they may have on other people. So far, I think Harold has brought back into the theatre well-honed words which are not pretentious, and are not gilded, and are not sequinned. I think he has brought poetic drama back into the theatre. I don't know whether he would admit it, but it does seem to me that the path that Edward Bond has followed has in some sense been prepared by Pinter. They're very different, but there's a similar precision in the use of language, the sense of rhythm, the concrete use of images. On the other hand, the surface of Pinter has been disaster to countless television plays. I'm bored stiff with cross-talk, and people misunderstanding and non-communicating, but you can't blame Harold for that. That's imitating the surface.

Is there such a thing as a Pinter world-view?

Oh, Christ. Speaking personally, I get a very bleak, very uncompromising, very hostile view of life out of him. Counterbalanced by a longing for contact and relation and . . . not getting into a situation of deep regrets, which is very painful. Because all his characters do have regrets, do crucify themselves, and everybody else. But I think what is for me wonderful about Pinter is that in an unblinkingly hostile situation where everybody does go wrong in some way or another, there are little moments of light and tenderness which are cherished. He is a very pessimistic dramatist: but I don't really understand how anybody could honestly be writing in the 1960s or 1970s and be particularly sunny. People are always saying to me, 'Why don't you do happy plays, that are life-enhancing?' to which the answer is, 'Well, why don't people write them?' But I find the great thing about him is that his tenderness and his compassion are not sentimental, but absolutely, unblinkingly accurate.

Nor cynical . . .

Not at all, he's not cynical, he's unblinking. He scrutinises life unyieldingly, and I think my job as a director is to scrutinise it, if I can, as carefully as he has.

Barry Foster

Barry Foster (1931-2002) studied with Pinter at Central School of Speech and Drama, and acted with him in Ireland in the 1950s in Anew McMaster's company. He remained a close friend of Pinter for the rest of his life. His first role in a Pinter play was that of Albert Stokes, in the premiere of A Night Out *in 1960 on the BBC. He went on to act as Mick in a revival of* The Caretaker, *in the TV premiere of* Tea Party *and* The Basement *in 1970, as Deeley in the BBC film of* Old Times *in 1975, in* A Slight Ache *in 1987, in* Night School *in 1998, and in* Mountain Language *and the premiere of* Party Time *in 1991.*

How did you first meet Harold Pinter?

We met through my wife Judith, at Central School. Harold first introduced himself to Judith saying he was a poet. There was no hint of writing a play in those days. We were all writing poetry at Central, and Harold's was quite difficult, surreal stuff.

I mean, I think all his writing is from a poetic source. Nothing is planned. There is no grid reference, there is no graph made of it, and where the climax will come and what the thesis is. There isn't a thesis. Well, really there is, but it sometimes takes years to discover. He doesn't set out to prove it step by step.

He's written some good poems. But I think his most successful poems are his plays.

After that, Harold went to Ireland to work with Mac, where he got his *real* training. Of course we exchanged letters throughout the time he was there, and he wrote one saying, 'He's looking for another actor, and I recommended you.' And of course, Mac loved what Harold did. They got on like houses on fire. So just on Harold's say-so he hired me, without even seeing me! I think he was slightly horrified when this rather short, red-haired number turned up. But I'd studied it all, and so I zoomed away, and we had a fantastic six months there.

Is Pinter's essay on Mac a fair account of what it was like?

Oh, absolutely! In fact, when he was writing it we talked together about it all. I was there when Mac said to the cow, 'No autographs today, dear!' And the 'buckets' instead of 'ducats' in *The Merchant of Venice*! That's absolutely true!

Were you onstage for that?

Oh yes! I was Lorenzo, who isn't in the court scene, of course, he's back at Belmont. And so you throw a cloak over your head and you become an old woman or an old man in the court scene: you're in the crowd. And Harold said 'Buckets' instead of 'Ducats'. And then Mac said, 'If every bucket were in six parts and every part a bucket, I would have my bond.' And so when that happened, the entire court – with the exception of the Doge, who is up centre on a big chair and can't move – all the rest of us were completely corpsing, laughing so much we just sauntered off! We just sort of walked upstage and disappeared into the wings! No one could hack it! And Harold was left with Mac down centre. And with Mac glaring at him about two feet over him, as he describes: 'Grave like an eagle'. One thing Harold doesn't mention is that he was never very good at corpsing. He always used to hold his nose! And he looked upstage, holding his nose! He seemed to think, 'They'll never notice if I do that – the whole audience are totally beguiled by that!'

What do you think Mac liked about Pinter's acting?

Well, he'd got the right sort of dark, saturnine, dangerous romance that was right up Mac's street, you know, coming from pre-First World War and post-post-First World War classical acting and so on. And of course Harold's magnificent voice! All that was right up his street. He's become a consummate actor now. None of us were then.

What was Pinter like as Iago?

Oh, his Iago was positively devilish!

Devilishly good?

No, I mean he was *dressed* like him, he was dressed like Mephistopheles! You know, with the high black collar, big cloak, everything. I mean, that was Mac's style – it was the style of the time.

But it worked?

Oh yes. *Brilliantly.* I mean – probably we would now call it a bit 'over-illustrated' . . . But it was thrilling, and Mac loved it. And of course also Harold brought to it a scholarship and a love of the work, that Mac wasn't used to in his Irish company!

And Mac welcomed his natural command. And in as much as I could provide the same sort of thing, he welcomed that. Mac wanted someone to hit the ball low and fast over the net, so that he could play *his* shots, you know. He didn't want some guy who can't even say hello on the other side of the stage! Not like his contemporary, Wolfit, who famously would play Lear convinced that the sea captain at the end was going to steal the play from him!

Presumably Mac could hold his own, even against Pinter's Iago?

Mac? As Othello? Iago's got no chance! He could have Jesus
Christ playing that part, and he'd still have no chance! And
that was the wonderful thing about working for Mac,
because he encouraged us to be as powerful as we possibly
could! Unlike these other guys, who had their spotlights,
who had their own bit of snow falling on them and everything, everyone else pushed into the Stygian corners of the
stage! None of that with Mac!

And when it was your turn, with Harold as Iago, or Pauline
Flanagan playing Portia in *Merchant of Venice*, Mac turned
upstage below them, and said, 'It's your turn – do it!' So it
was a wonderful school for us to learn in. Harold – and
anyone else with any sense – grabbed hold of it with both
hands.

*So you're saying that, though he doesn't mention it himself in the
essay, Pinter was something of a favourite son of Mac?*

Oh, I think so. Yes. Mac would have thought, probably,
'Here's my successor.'

*And did you imagine that was what he was going to do, or what
you were going to do?*

Yes! We used to sit around in pubs, long after the shows. It
was the way – *is* the way – in Ireland. Sometimes on a market day you didn't start *Hamlet* until nine o'clock at night,
you know. If you did, they wouldn't come in! And they were
all drunk; you had to fight for their attention! The curtain
would come down on *Hamlet* at about quarter to one, and
then we'd be in the bar, with the priests and all the rest of
them there, having a drink. Pauline and Harold and myself,
and a chap called Max Ettlinger, who became a priest. We'd
sit around saying, 'What's going to happen to us?' We thought

we were all going to go to Stratford, which was the summit of success to us. We would have people read our palms, anything, anything! Grab hold of anything, to know just how famous we were going to be.

So we all tried an audition for Stratford and got nowhere at all, and we all were interviewed for Wolfit when we got back, and only Harold got in. He got to carry a spear and say a couple of lines in Wolfit's company at the King's Hammersmith. And I certainly didn't. Alan Owen, a Welsh playwright to be, was in with Harold in Wolfit's company.

But then Harold's plays happened. You know how he had the idea for *The Room*, don't you? At this party. Where he met my wife! In Earl's Court somewhere, or past the Cromwell Road. Someone said, 'You've got to come downstairs.' He went down, and there was this blue-rinsed, made-up guy with an apron on, cooking, frying meat for this huge bloke, who said nothing. And he was rabbiting away; and it was Quentin Crisp. He was the woman. He is the woman in *The Room*.

A Night Out was the first thing I ever did of his, on radio, and then I did *The Caretaker*, playing Mick, directed by Michael Bakewell.

What sort of a bloke is Mick?

Well, I thought a lot of people missed the point about Mick until Harold played it for a while, in the first big production with Donald Pleaseance as Davies, about 1962-3. It was freezing, snow all over the place. Alan Bates [playing Mick] was off for a while, I think probably filming something or other. Harold took over for a few weeks. And he got it. He got the pain in Mick. I'd never seen anyone do that before. And it was good.

Where does the pain come from?

I think it's to do with his brother. I mean, it's not what's in
the front of the character . . . When you sit and read it, you
think, 'Oh, this is a flash geezer! He's on top, he's a winner!
He knows what he's doing. He's an operator.' But everything he's doing, in fact he's doing for his brother. And his
brother, shall we say, unwittingly rejects him; Aston says,
'No, no, I want this old guy to come.'

It's not that he says that he rejects Mick, but out of the
goodness of his heart he asks Davies in, and in a way that's
a threat to Mick. Emotionally, not physically, and hence
Mick's vacuum-cleaner terrorising.

And then his speech about decorating the house comes from
the same source. And that becomes a sort of *Vogue*-maga-
zine rundown of what's going to happen. It's coming from
Vogue and *House and Garden* of the time, the late fifties. It's
very post-Festival of Britain. And he's lifted that into this
great aria that actually is a poetic expression of his care for
his brother! It's a bravura show-off speech – great stuff for
an actor to get his teeth into. And it's got intimidation in it
as well. And it's all gobbledy-gook as far as Davies is concerned. But why is he doing it? Why does he want to do up
this wretched old place? He's got his own place somewhere
else, hasn't he? He's doing it for his brother. And Harold
showed me that, he got to the heart of the pain Mick feels at
the threat of his brother not accepting it.

Towards the end – in the beginning of the last movement, as
it were, when the two brothers are on the stage – Harold
writes, 'They smile.' That reminds you that these are brothers.
And one is clearly mortally wounded, and can't cope except
with a screwdriver and an old bit of electrical equipment,
and the other could run the country. But he wants to do
something for his brother instead, and his brother bloody

well isn't taking it on! It's quite difficult to do, because the last thing you want is a sweetly sentimental thing that never happens between brothers. It's not that. It's just a very precious moment.

There are similar crucial moments in other plays. If you miss those moments, then you are perplexed by the plays, I think.

Well, a lot of people are. They say, 'It's a con. And my boy of six could do this.' It's because they haven't made the connections. It's like Picasso. The same people think Picasso's a con, and their boy of six could paint just as well.

Deeley, the man in *Old Times*, is, I think, the response of the intelligent, non-university person, shall we say, with non-affluent beginnings, to having emerged into a world where he's surrounded by posers and *poseurs*. Then, in this play, he meets his match with the woman from the past. And he finishes up in a kind of delirium, going back to his old days, with friends around Paddington Library and all that. He's really exhausted, he's been beaten to a pulp by this woman. When I was playing the part I thought there was a sort of an echo of the parties that we went to in those days. Even that party where Harold met Judith and Quentin Crisp. So it's a sort of strange, dreamlike revisitation of my student days, and of that time. By the end, Deeley's had the guts knocked out of him. The part of the wife becomes central, her intelligence, her beauty . . . She's a magnet. They're revolving around her, and she just *is*. She is ontological! She's *it*.

How about your part in Party Time?

Of course, the thesis of the play is perfectly apparent, and my part encapsulates the kind of establishment brutality that gets Harold in such a lather – and gets us *all* in such a lather. I had a fairly straight, simple line to pursue there, as a man with total power. The enjoyable thing in the piece was that he didn't need to exercise any brute power at all, or only the very faintest flash, so one could indulge in Harold's poetry with the sort of oblique references that he does so well. I had one little speech to Peter Howitt, who was playing a younger character that I despised. I tell him about the health club and how they use towels to remove 'all the blackheads' from your nose. He's powerful so he is able to talk about blackheads and the amusing art of squeezing them! These apparent non-sequiturs all have a tremendous poetic force. And later, in front of the character played by Peter Howard, who's really got up my nose by now, I engage Dotty [Dorothy] Tutin in a discussion about forks – just the sound of the word 'fork' is something you can use to enormous effect. And of course it leaves the Peter Howitt character saying, 'What the hell is going on here!'

He's bemused, yet he has the strong feeling that someone just called him a blackhead, you'd say?

Exactly so.

Of course, a lot of these plays are political in a deep sense. *The Birthday Party*, obviously. But they weren't seen that way at the time. People like Tynan were saying, 'Harold, I don't know how characters in your plays would vote!'

And what did Pinter say?

I don't know. He probably said, 'Oh God, fuck off!' Oh, he said something like, 'I write about people who are sitting in a room, and someone opens the door, and the question is: do they come in or don't they? And if they come in and shut the door, what happens then? I'm writing about the circumstances people are in before they can get up, go out and vote, before they've voted.'

When you guys were growing up in the fifties, it seems to me that, to put it bluntly, there was nobody to vote for.

Well, there was something to vote for in '45. After that, things got more complicated. In the 1940s (and later in the fifties) I was reading the Left Book Club books, with the yellow covers, Michael Foot and those people. I was working in a lab then, at EMI, and the guys in the lab, who were older than me, would say, 'You read that for a start!' Politics, Chinese poetry and philosophy, and everything. They were feeding me all this stuff. I had a fantastic education in a laboratory in EMI!

And did you feel proud of the achievements of the '45 Labour government?

Absolutely! The achievements were enormous. National Health Service. And plenty of other things, too.

What about the common perception that the so-called Angry Young Men of the fifties felt there was no cause left to fight for? The notion that you were intellectually engaged, you thought that politics were important, that art and culture were important; and yet there was some sort of vacuum. There was nothing to kick against.

In retrospect, it was not unlike now, in a way: now everyone despairs of Blair. Now we've got two Tory parties. Blair's is a Tory government. In '45 it was red-hot: you know, 'This is the new order, the new world order! We're going to change everything!' 'We are the masters now,' Shawcross said. And what happened to Shawcross? He became a bloody Tory! By 1955 we just weren't interested in politics in the way we had been. We thought, 'Politicians? Sod the lot,' you know? I think it was the inner life that we were concerned about.

So when Pinter's early plays were written, that must have been incredibly exciting to you as a way of delineating that inner life.

Yeah. To us. Though to the general public, I have to tell you, it was meaningless rubbish! Until, to his undying credit, Mr Hobson said, 'This man's talking sense.'

You said that Pinter directed your finest performance. What was that?

Yes, I played Hamlet early on, on television – schools' television. I did a total of three hours in six episodes. At the time I thought, 'Well, that's about twice what Sir Laurence did on screen.' We did all the soliloquies, for example! And it was lit like a first feature movie. I thought, 'This is the highlight of my career.'

. . . Until Harold offered me Simon Gray's script of *The Rear Column* and the part of Major Bartlett. And that was a big hurdle. I trained for it, and I think I cleared it with a few inches to spare. And Harold thought so too, and he wrote me a very great letter afterwards. I felt that Simon's incredible gift, writing this piece, Harold's perception in directing it, and my take on how to embody it – all those three things came together and I was intensely proud of it. And then it collapsed, forced to close after five weeks, thanks largely to Bernard Levin and one or two other critics. It was a tremendous play, absolutely devastating. A faultless cast including Jeremy Irons and Simon Ward. Which was Harold's doing, of course, in picking the actors.

How did Pinter get the best out of you as an actor?

Well, I really don't know. I had a view on the thing, and I pursued it, and he guided me in the right way. But then perhaps that's the best way to direct an actor; when he thinks he's just being left to do it. My feeling was that he left me to it, but that can't have been so.

You must be immensely proud that the two of you have been friends and have shared the same zeitgeist.

I don't know if 'proud' is the word. I'm immensely privileged that, that grey autumn in the common room in the Albert Hall, when I started on my little course at Central School, there was this dark-haired young man who I started talking to. I feel immensely privileged that I was around. I sometimes think he's written the plays, and the poetry, actually, that I wanted to write . . .

Susan Engel

Susan Engel was one of the first actors ever to perform Pinter's work. As a drama student at Bristol University she created Rose in The Room *in 1957. She was directed by Pinter in the film of Simon Gray's* Butley *in 1971, and has played Pauline in* A Kind of Alaska *both on television (in 1984) and on stage (in 1985).*

When did you first encounter Harold Pinter?

I was an undergraduate at Bristol University when Henry Woolf was there doing a post-graduate course. And we were good mates, mainly on account of the fact that I'm about six foot tall, and he's not quite as tall as that. Henry one day said, and this is the way Henry talks, 'I've got a mate who writes a bit, and he never finishes anything and if I could get him to finish some little piece, I've told him, there's a studio at Bristol for the students, we've got access to a studio and we've got free time, if you've got free time – would you have free time and do you want to come in with me?' For weeks it went on, 'If I get him to finish it, will you do it?' I'd say, 'So, how's your friend doing with our play?' And he'd say, 'Oh, don't – I couldn't get him to send it to me. You know, he, he just can't get it together.' Then finally one day he got it, on a few bits of very badly typed, cheap typing paper. And it was *The Room*. I still have my copy, with Harold's annotations.

So, Henry cast us, and we rehearsed, and played it at the end of term. I suppose it could have happened another way, but the way Henry played Mr Kidd, I mean, it *was* Henry. It was obviously written for him.

I was all of nineteen, and we thought the whole thing was a fantastic experience, because never before had one had that kind of a script. We weren't professional actors. We were studying, and what I knew about drama at that moment was about Giraudoux and Anouilh. We never studied contemporary fifties drama like Priestley or Somerset Maugham. That wasn't on the cards.

So, *The Room* was unlike anything one had encountered before, but, apart from students, who thought it was great, and a few aficionados whose eyes were wide, the academics at Bristol didn't like it. I don't know if they even sat through it. It was not in any way an event for the grown-ups, if you know what I mean, and in fact we weren't given any help, or any money. We'd almost beg the department, 'Can we please have a chair, and could we have a kettle?' 'No, you can get your own.'

But then we did it again for the Student Drama Festival, and all the professors at the university, all the grown-ups and the theatre people said, 'Oh, it's fascinating.'

It was in Bristol that Pinter was introduced to Jimmy Wax. Were you associated with Jimmy Wax?

After I left Bristol University, I was in the Bristol Old Vic School for a year, and then I went into the Bristol Old Vic Company – it was my first job. We were doing a play by John Hall, and on the first night his agent came down. I, being very green and provincial, thought that, coming from London, this agent is an agent with a capital A. Now it so happened that Harold – who of course I knew a bit by then – was on tour in Bristol, and I had put him up. He was sleeping on a mattress in a room downstairs in the big house where I lived. So I went to the first-night party, and I met this agent Jimmy Wax – who was just a wonderful man – and I said to him, 'Why don't you come back up with me to Clifton where I live, because down on the floor below me, on a mattress, is sleeping a guy called Harold Pinter, and he needs an agent.' Because I thought Harold was a great playwright. It was the sort of thing you wouldn't dream of daring to do when you grow up.

So we went back up the road, and we woke Harold up and I said, 'Oh, you've got to come and have a cup of tea and meet this guy. He's an agent.' And that's how he met Jimmy. They talked all night and, and we read a little bit of *The Room* on the little kitchen table there, for Jimmy, and Jimmy took it on, just like that.

Back in the 1970s a friend of mine, Michael Burrell, rang me up, and said that he'd got some money from the British Council, and did I want to go with him to Morocco, and do a tour of the Moroccan universities, acting out bits of the set plays? Well, I said, 'Great.' I was out of work. February, lovely time to go to Morocco. So we went round the universities of Morocco – Rabat, Casablanca, Marrakech, Fez – and they would say, 'Could you do scenes from the Scottish play, a bit of *Coriolanus*, a bit of this and a bit of that and, and a modern play or two – Shaw, perhaps?' And we decided to do something from *The Birthday Party*, as a modern play, and then we would talk to the students afterwards.

This was the period just before fundamentalism had arrived, and the students were very, very interesting. They all knew their Shakespeare extremely well, but they didn't know anything about Harold Pinter – except what had arrived on their bookshelves. They had tomes on Absurdism, British Absurdism in the 1960s, and then they had us, acting *The Birthday Party*.

We had to take our own teapot, because they had different kinds of teapots, the Moroccans – they don't have teapots like a Pinter type. And we had to take a box of cornflakes, because they wouldn't have known what a box of cornflakes was for. So we had these props, commonplace to us but strange to them. And it was a bit like we were creatures from outer space, because they knew about Harold Pinter from the books that they had studied, but not from live performance.

So they would ask questions afterwards: 'Do you think that the Absurdism of *The Birthday Party* corresponds to the Absurdist element?' And I remember sitting there in front of this bank of students and saying, 'Look at the script and the play and what it's about. As far as Absurdism goes, just wipe your hands free, wash your mouths out with soap and water. Fuck Absurdism!' We were almost given the sack in that particular university because these students had to pass exams, and the exam questions that their professors gave them were exactly the questions they were asking. I just found that very sad.

As soon as there's a gap in expectations, people fill it with a term like Absurdism. So when you got this script of The Room, *and it was enigmatic, difficult . . .*

No, I don't find any of Harold's work enigmatic. You just have to sit on a London bus to see that conversation is enigmatic because you've missed what they said at the stop before. That's how conversations are in life. I just felt, here's somebody who talks like what we talk like. If something is full of meaning, it's full of meaning because of what the character has thought of before – which, if you're a good actor, you fill out as a character. But it doesn't come from anything but the character.

Harold is sent up because of his pauses and because of the meticulousness of his writing. Well, it is meticulous, in the same way Shakespeare is meticulous, and if you destroy the verse, you're not doing it right. 'Speak the speech as I set it down for you.' That's all; and you don't improvise. You just follow what's in the script. You do Rose Hudd [in *The Room*] as he's written her, and you stop when he says stop and you make the tea when he says you make the tea. 'She rises, pours tea at the table,' and she does.

I have heard actors say that the thing about Pinter's work is that it's opaque and elliptical and it's impossible to know what's going on – and that it's therefore more important for actors to attend to the music of the lines . . .

The music of the lines is in every play. Of course, if you're speaking them as they're written, then they will have a rhythm, and Harold's rhythms are not the same as Somerset Maugham's rhythms. Or the same as Shakespeare's rhythms. They're his rhythms and a lot of them come from characters who may have an Irish or a Jewish background – a working-class background – it's the rhythm of Hackney, perhaps, in some characters.

When you first read The Room *did it strike you as an authentic English speech?*

I find it completely and totally authentic. It's so simple, 'This is a good room.' Full stop. The character of Mr Kidd, for instance – that's the way Henry talks as well. There are a lot of Jewish inflections, and there are a lot of Hackney inflections, and if you abide by the script, you can't help but do them.

But I see absolutely nothing elliptical. There's nothing that is weird to understand. And it seems funny that some people think otherwise! They're not listening. They're not watching. Until '57, working-class characters, or Irish characters – anyone who wasn't middle-class and English was written patronisingly, because they weren't written by working-class writers. I mean, take Doolittle, the dustman in Shaw's *Pygmalion*: he's nothing like how a Doolittle might actually talk. Then after John Osborne, working-class writers suddenly flooded the English stage, but until *Look Back in Anger* I can't think of any working-class characters that were not written by middle-class writers in a patronising way.

Harold emerged right in the middle of this revolution. But one thing that's interesting about Harold is that he has not remained imprisoned by his working-class origins, as I think quite a lot of the Royal Court writers did. Where the working-class element comes into his writing is in the musicality of the verbs and the nouns and the full stops that they use. Whereas Wesker, for example, is a social realist working-class writer – he is encapsulated in that area, which is why, whenever he's tried to kind of get away from that, he writes rather bad plays. He only writes well about what he knows – which is his family and those Norfolk people. But Harold's gone way beyond that.

One thing that Henry Woolf wished to emphasise was the importance of Yiddish culture for Pinter.

Well, I was introduced to Harold through Henry, and Henry practically talks Yiddish. Most of our conversation together is full of Yiddishisms, so I can't help but approach Harold's writing, his early writing I mean, as home. But there's lots of places later where that doesn't happen at all. There aren't any Jews in a lot of his plays, and there aren't any of those Jewish inflections in a lot of his plays.

Give me a Jewish inflection – an example.

Mr Kidd talks about his mum, 'I think my mum was a Jewess,' he says. Then, 'She didn't have many babies . . . ' Jewish mums are supposed to have hundreds of babies. Mr

Kidd's admitting to being Jewish, but at the same time trying to talk about the Jews in the way the Gentiles do, because he's talking to non-Jews.

I like it when he says, 'I was her senior . . . She had a lovely boudoir.'

Yes! *'Beautiful boudoir . . . '* It strikes me as the love of a working-class person for a new word, and it is a lovely word. I was born in Vienna, my family are Viennese, part of the Jewish bourgeoisie, and the thing is, it was fashionable to make little Frenchisms, you know, the Yiddish Jews would try to imitate the bourgeois Viennese, and the bourgeoisie loved talking a bit of French. We found it divinely funny, the words Yiddish people used to sound posh. We were young and stupid then, but Harold and Henry still, when they write to me, use a bit of Yiddish. There's a joy in language, and there's a joy in imitating for Jews. They're very good at quoting from the Bible, the Talmud, and quotations have a very important place in Jewish culture. I don't think Harold's parents were particularly religious, they didn't keep the Sabbath and all that, and after all, there aren't many Jewish characters in Harold's plays, but the attitude remains, the sense that it is part of everyday life to use strange words, the words of others.

What do you think of Pinter's writing for and about women?

Well, they're fully rounded, real and interesting people, with hearts. They have a sense of the meaning and the purpose of life, so their place in the cosmos has great value and importance. I think it demeans them to say that they are of a certain type, or that they're Pinteresque characters, because they are so diverse as well. They're not all Vivien [Merchant], and you don't have to play them all as Vivien, if you see what I mean, though she did play them rather well. And she had good legs and she crossed them rather wonderfully.

Everybody talks about her role in shaping and defining these parts.

Yes, obviously she did. A few of Harold's female characters, like any playwright's characters, are totally influenced by females that Harold has known; Vivien was an inspiration for him. When they started off, she was the star, and she was a brilliant actress – with the same repertory training and background as Harold. She was very striking, very conscious of her sexuality, predatory perhaps, a sort of Cleopatra.

Speaking of the fact that Pinter did all this work acting in repertory companies, can you, as an actor, see that in his writing?

Yes, from the point of view that I think he knows what a good entrance and a good exit speech is. I mean, that's what good writing, good drama is – it's to do with the rhythm. He's also a very good director because he knows how actors want to behave. I played the wife in the film of *Butley* that he directed.

He's not intimidating, as a director of actors, I mean?

Oh no. He's one of us. He's an actor, so you long for him to give you notes. I think he is a seminal director for actors – as long as the actors don't revere him or are frightened of him, and there's no reason why they need to be because he's actually very humble, very respectful of other actors. I mean, all a director can do is to tell you when you're false, to make sure that you're doing the script right, and to tell you if you're playing a false note. If the actors are good, he knows how to help them.

Roger Lloyd Pack

Roger Lloyd Pack's first Pinter stage role was that of Joey in
The Homecoming *in 1978, although prior to that he acted in
the Pinter-scripted film* The Go-Between *in 1971. In 1984 he
created the part of Victor in* One for the Road *(a part he later
played in a BBC film), and played the Controller in* Victoria
Station. *In 1991 he acted in the premiere of* Party Time, *and
in* Mountain Language. *In 1997 he acted alongside Pinter in*
Look, Europe!, *and in 2000 he played Mick in a ten-minute
extract from* The Caretaker, *in the context of a platform
performance at the National Theatre, with Pinter taking the
role of Aston.*

I saw you in the platform performance of The Caretaker *playing Mick opposite Pinter's Aston. Are there any plans to do more
with that?*

No, I don't think so! I'm a bit old to play Mick, really. And
Harold, I suppose, is a bit old to play Aston! I was delighted
to play Mick though, because it means that I've played every
part in it – I know that play entirely. I had already understudied Mick, and I've played Aston and Davies.

I also understudied Aston at the Mermaid Theatre, as a
young actor, when Leonard Rossiter was Davies. John Hurt
was Mick, and Jeremy Kemp was Aston. It's important to
me because when I saw *The Caretaker* first in 1960, I was
knocked over by it, like many people. It affirmed what I
liked about theatre, and I thought, 'Well, this is it. Now I
understand.' I just thought it was a wonderful comedy, a
hilarious piece of writing.

The theatre of the time was John Osborne, *Look Back In Anger,* and Ionesco. John Osborne's piece was obviously groundbreaking, but seemed to me a bit didactic, to be honest. So when I saw *The Caretaker* I felt that this was what I wanted from theatre, really. And the humour of it, I love the humour of it.

You weren't one of the people who thought, 'Ah, this is a very serious, studied piece?'

I've never approached Harold's work in that way, even then as a sixteen-year-old schoolboy, I just thought it was a wonderful black comedy. And he was the first writer, for me anyway, to reflect how people actually spoke – the pauses, these famous pauses, are just an observation of how people speak.

So, as a young actor, you came across Pinter's work . . .

He was just a heroic figure to me. I know he'd be embarrassed to be thought of as a heroic figure, but he *was*, at that age. I just got everything he'd written, and read everything, and at drama school did sketches, and wrote in his style.

How did he come across as a person?

He was terribly kind. My wife was dressing his wife at the time, Vivien Merchant, at Stratford. And Vivien thought that my wife would make a very good secretary for Harold. And at some point I went to Hanover Terrace and met Harold. I was just awestruck, really, but he was very kind to me, and very friendly, actually. I was rather impressed that he took me seriously as a person, when I was only a sort of rather callow youth.

So who was the first Pinter character that you played?

The first Pinter play I was in was at drama school, I played Stanley in *The Birthday Party*. Robert Shaw had played Stanley, and he was a very strong man and rather good. But I wasn't. I was very thin and – I'm sure – rather paranoid myself at the time. And I was able to enter into what it must have been like to be Stanley quite easily. I had been – not tremendously bullied – but I had experienced, as a kid playing in bombsites, being intimidated by a couple of older lads.

For Stanley I needed to know what type of music he played, and what kind of background he came from, what his upbringing had been like . . . I'm always interested in what kind of babyhood, childhood, a character's had.

My first professional Pinter role was Joey in *The Home-coming*, first of all at the Leeds Playhouse, and then at the Garrick Theatre in the West End for six months. You could imagine Joey as completely denied everything. As a child I imagined he didn't get much, he was completely ignored – bullied, probably, as the youngest in the family. And that helped to give a kind of truth to his stupidity, and also raised the question of whether it's not just stupidity, but a way of survival.

You created Victor in One for the Road, *didn't you? Bearing in mind what you said about Osborne, what do you feel about the polemical nature of Pinter's 'political' later plays?*

I have been in all three of his overtly political plays. *One for the Road* was really a study in tyranny, but very internal, about one man. Although I didn't speak much as Victor, the part requires a lot of work. I remember going to these dynamic meditations that were around at the time, where a group of people just screamed and shouted; it was a sort of therapy thing. I went to them because I wanted to know what it felt like to be someone who would have screaming around them all day, to have that sort of washed-out feeling of deadness, and yet to contribute in some way. Because Victor was onstage in a small space, he was a powerful presence; I wanted to be able to convey the fact that he'd been beaten about and wanted that to be believable.

Of course I also built a history around Victor. I imagined a literary career. You need to bring something on with you so that you can inhabit the character.

And did you do that for, say, Davies?

It was quite hard with Davies. Where had Davies come from? What was his life before? He's just a one-off eccentric character. And yet I'd met characters like Davies, who just come up to you, and you wonder what sort of plane they're living on. I also thought of people that I knew. One very educated man in particular, who was completely tripped-out, who had had ECT – a brilliant man, but an alcoholic and unable to conform in any way or – or lead a conventional life.

So you imagined that Davies might have been an educated man?

No. But I think he's an intelligent man, very clever – sly, cunning and sort of ruthless, unscrupulous. It was more his quicksilver mind that I fished out from this bloke. He's such a huge part, too, he's a tour de force of writing.

You say he's intelligent and sly . . . What's likeable about him, do you think?

Very little! But I think he has got to have something likeable about him; at least he has to engage the sympathy of the audience. He's got to have a certain amount of charm. Audiences just enjoy some characters. They don't really like him on the stage but quite enjoy watching him operate. In a

sort of appalled way, they can't believe that kind of unscrupulous behaviour, the way he ruthlessly plays one person off against the other. And yet he is a victim of society, in
a sense, he's on the scrapheap, and he's not completely all
there, he can't keep it together. I suppose that gives an
audience some sympathy. Also, I don't know how much I'm
endeared to him because of the writing, because of his
humour. He's one of the great comic characters of our literature – he has airs and graces, and he imagines himself to be
more than he is. 'I've had dinner with the best of them, I've
been there!' His pretensions! His pretensions to grandeur
are laughable!

And the shoes!

The shoes! He has to set himself up as an expert on shoes
that he, a man in his position, would turn down. It's because
he can't accept them, it's because he's too proud. It's terribly true this – he knows there's something wrong with
Aston, and the fact that he will be receiving a gift from Aston
would make him indebted to Aston, which he couldn't bear
to be. Aston's the only one who's likeable, who you have
some sympathy for.

*Perhaps you could say something about the particular demands
on an actor of Pinter's use of language – you described it as stylised,
poetic and yet incredibly true to life.*

Harold's writing is very beautiful, very rhythmical. And the
rhythms of speech are absolutely critical to each part. I'm
always very respectful of writers' intentions, but I've never
felt I've got to be so precise about inflections as I am with
Harold's work; what weight you give one word rather than
another, how much weight you give to a phrase.

There is a sort of internal logic to the speech of each
character, which you have to be true to. You have to find the

logic of the character, what his world is, and be true to that. And in performance you can't make any comment upon that character; you have to act according to your instinctive sense of that logic. It's terrible to overplay Pinter – to say the line as if it's got huge import.

Pinter directed you in Party Time. *What would you say his strengths are as a director?*

Well, he understands the process of acting . . . And he allows you to find your own way into a character. He's very good at making sure that you find the humanity in a character, that you're not carried away with the language, and that you don't separate the language from the character.

The very opposite, in fact, of the controlling director of popular cliché?

The very opposite. Although in *Party Time*, I have to say he was more insistent on inflection. He knew how he wanted the lines said, and sometimes he would say, 'I don't think the writer would agree with you.' Whereas before he was more prepared to allow the performance to come out of *you*, and develop. He's always been very generous in that way as a director.

What are his other strengths?

Well, the best thing a director can do is to let you get on with it, but be there to help you to do what you're finding difficult, and guide you into places. The ideal is to let you feel that you 'own' the part. And a lot of directors will take away ownership from you, in all sorts of little ways, you know, 'I think you should do it like this' or 'I want you to do it here,' so that when you come to play it, you'll remember that note. An actor has to own the part, and the director's job really is to help him do that. And not a lot of directors know that: they're very keen on imposing themselves on you. Harold, because he's an actor, understands the process of creating a performance, and the importance of owning it.

Is there anything else that you think is important about Pinter that should be said?

Well, I think that he's a major writer, and a serious presence in the theatre, a standard-bearer, I suppose. He's a real man of the theatre in that he understands the theatre in a sort of grassroots way, but then at the same time he's able to engage in important issues. After all, theatre's only acting, you know, and it's only make-believe. But he's taken his beliefs into the political arena, and he'll stand up and be counted. He's fearless – he's a fearless person, which in our business is quite a rarity.

Roger Davidson

Roger Davidson has appeared in several Pinter plays, including the first productions of The Hothouse *and* One for the Road. *He has also been a good friend of Pinter for more than twenty years. Davidson represents the theatrical generation following Pinter's own, who grew up regarding him in many ways as a leader, and he says that he is still surprised to think that he has come to work with Pinter. A notable feature of the interview is how his expectations differed from the reality of working with him.*

I first came across Pinter's work when I went to drama school, in the late sixties, early seventies. He was my idol. I thought it was wonderful stuff, and I, of course, like everybody else who fancied himself, directed the obligatory performances of *The Dumb Waiter* and *The Birthday Party*. We all wrote theses on him, dissected everything. I was very much into the idea of Pinter as Absurdist, out of the school of Beckett, Ionesco and the rest.

What did you like about the writing?

Well, the whole thing: it had such singularity of language, such singularity of vision. At that time, we were all going around in black polo-neck sweaters being Existentialists, and I thought that Harold was coming from the same place and had absolutely got it on the button! I now think that was a fairly trite kind of way of boxing him in – it's a mistake to put him into an Absurdist school, because he's bigger than that.

But I loved the stuff for other reasons, too. I loved the language, and I loved the formality. There was a fixed, centred and artistic formality about all the work, despite that sense you also get of randomness in events.

When did you first meet or work with Pinter?

When I got the part in *The Hothouse* in 1980, which was a play that he'd written in 1958, I think, but had then put away in a bottom drawer.

I think he felt, having dug the play out and read it totally fresh, through the perspective of twenty-odd years, that there were absolutely clear threads in *The Hothouse* of political oppression and authoritarianism, and of the themes which increasingly had come to the fore in his writing and his public persona by the eighties.

I don't think he changed anything much of it. He maybe took a couple of lines out here and there. But effectively – and this in large measure holds true of all his work, from what he's said to me about it – he writes it, and there it is. He very rarely seems to rewrite his plays when they're done. And we did *The Hothouse* in 1980, twenty-odd years after it was written, almost word for word as it was written then.

I was absolutely thrilled, of course, to be in the first production, because I'd always revered Pinter. And suddenly, bingo! Here I was, not only going to be *in* the first production of a hitherto unperformed Harold Pinter, but directed by the man himself!

Who were you playing?

Well, in all the plays that I did of Harold's, I ended up playing victims. And it started with this character called Lamb in *The Hothouse*, who was a small cog in a big institutional machine, who probably had ideas above his station in terms of what he saw his future as within the organisation, but alas was destined for a terrible homecoming of his own! He becomes a sacrificial lamb to the slaughter: he becomes the fall guy.

One understands that *The Hothouse*, the institution, contains a lot of very strange 'patients', so called, and they're all kept very much under lock and key. And it's the job of the aforementioned Lamb to be the lock-keeper and go around with a big bunch of keys, checking all the locks. The mayhem that emerges at the end, where all the staff bar one are slaughtered by the inmates, is held to be Lamb's responsibility, because he seemed to be absent on the night it happened. He *was* in fact absent on the night it happened, because he'd been put through a fairly convulsive treatment of shock therapy which had rendered him a complete cabbage.

When you played Lamb, did you base him on anybody that you knew or any kind of person that you'd met?

I'd emerged from drama school steeped in the Stanislavskian ethos of 'building a character from within'. I came out burning with the zeal to create in three dimensions everything I played. And here I was with Harold Pinter, and I assumed that Harold would think the same way as I did. So I was itching to know things like what Lamb's job was before he got the job with the institution that he was now with. And did he have one pair of slippers or did he have two? Was he an only child? All of that. Looking back, I went at it like a zealot! And I was very, very quickly disabused of all of that by Harold as director. He just looked at me in a rather puzzled way when I started to ask him all these questions, which at the time I thought were perfectly valid. I want to know is he an *arriviste*, has he been there for six months, has he been there two weeks and is desperate to impress somebody? But now I see that it was all abundantly clear from the words on the page.

So I was standing there wearing my Stanislavsky hat, and Harold basically knocked it off my head very quickly! He looked at me and he said, 'I don't think you need to know any of that. I think . . . When the door opens and he walks through the door, that's when you start to exist. I don't really go for any of this, "What happened at breakfast time",' he said. 'I don't think you need that. Just he walks through the door, and there he is.'

Once I sat down and got over being miffed about being told not to be so stupid, I realised he was right. I mean it's *always* good advice to tell an actor to concentrate on remembering his lines, walking through the door and not bumping into the furniture. But in Harold's plays it's especially good, because of the way they're written, and because all that he wants you to know is there in the writing, in the lines.

Were the other actors coming from the same point of view as you?

I was very much the new boy. I was the youngest member of the cast, the most recently trained, and the least experienced. I suspect the older members of the cast would have been doing an element of that for themselves as a matter of course anyway, but they didn't go on about it. They knew instinctively, which I didn't, that, 'Actually, this piece is funny, and let's worry about where the gags are a bit,' rather than, 'What's your motivation and what did you have for breakfast today?' They thought, 'How do we pace the scene? How do we give wing to what's on the page?'

I remember at one stage while we were rehearsing *The Hothouse* I was having a good time getting very serious about my interpretation, to the point where I was patently missing the *gags*, the jokes in the script. And Harold fixed me with a

quizzical stare and said, 'We are allowed to *laugh*, you know!
It is meant to be *funny* in places!'

When you talk to Harold it becomes clear very quickly that
he sees his plays as *comedies*; the laughs are very important.
But you have to remember that all the best comedy needs
truth. Subsequently, I played a lot of Ayckbourn in my career.
And if you play Ayckbourn with the notion that you're
going to be wildly funny and have the audience falling about
with laughter, you're probably destined to look like a prat. If
you play it as a bloke who desperately wants to sell a rather
ageing Morris Minor, or as a bloke who's had the day from
hell, *and* he feels terrible because he's having an affair . . . if
you play it for truth, if you play the characters truthfully, the
comedy comes out of what the writer has given you. If it's a
fine writer like Pinter, the jokes are there if you have a
rounded character to play.

*It sounds like you found yourself facing a paradox: you revered
Pinter as a modernist playwright, and then when you came to do
his work you found that his own acting training was indebted to
more classical traditions.*

The more I worked with Harold, the more I became aware
of just what a thoroughly grounded 'Man of the Theatre' he
was, essentially from the days when he toured Ireland with
Anew McMaster. Harold was first and foremost an actor,
and I don't think anybody should ever forget that. As a director, that gives him an enormous empathy and an enormous
kind of sense of collaborative sureness with actors. Because
he's *been* there, he *knows* what it's like, he knows what it's
like up there, and he knows how to help you out.

There is, in the nicest possible way, undoubtedly something
of the old ham in Harold. He understands the nature of the
craft of acting in weekly rep, and of simply standing there,
being able to tough it out when basically you hardly know

what you're going to say next! Sometimes you see his own plays or read them and at first sight it's almost like the rep actor's worst nightmare – as if they've *all* forgotten their lines and *nobody* knows what's going to happen next. But it never breaks down because Harold knows what it takes to make a piece hang together – he knows what will really work *in the theatre*, in front of an audience.

If you read his piece on McMaster, it's abundantly clear that he absolutely loves the classics. He loves Shakespeare, he loves Webster, and as a man of the theatre, he's absolutely rooted in that classical tradition. And again, he loved the old ham with an eye to the box office in McMaster. The actor-manager who hears that all the cinemas in Limerick are shut this week and says, 'What do we do? *We book Limerick!*' I mean, Harold's successful enough not to have to worry about audiences, but he doesn't despise them, or good old-fashioned principles of backsides on seats.

One of the great Pinter actors is Pinter himself. What do you most admire in Pinter's own acting?

I guess what I admire most is his absolute solidity in – in 'the being there'. I mean, there are parts that he was not born to play, parts that he's written himself that he was not born to play, there are parts that he absolutely *was* born to play. You know, he has a kind of elemental, animal force where he stands. It ties in again with his piece on McMaster. One thing Harold admires about McMaster's craft is that when he gets it right, he's absolutely four-square in the middle of the part, he is absolutely on the spine of it.

As he writes about McMaster, 'Dead in the centre of the role . . .'

Yeah, exactly. Harold at his best has that: he's absolutely in the bloody middle of it, and totally secure.

In the same sort of way, Harold's plays have a very pared-down, very clean, minimalist, stylised presentation. There is no extraneous movement. If somebody gets up and pours a drink, they get up and pour a drink for a purpose.

In rehearsals for *The Hothouse* I watched Harold giving us an example of what he wanted, as to the kind of pace that he wanted somebody to run up and down some stairs. And I thought, 'This absolutely accords with the kind of physical clarity of the shapes that he sees in his stage pictures.'

There's something very clear and very precise about the way Harold blocks plays. Now, some of his critics have said that it's too mechanical, that it isn't fluid. But in terms of how he would direct you to come through a door, proffer a cup of coffee to somebody, pour that cup of coffee, give it to her, sit down in a chair opposite her, it was all part of the physical expression of the musical score. It's been a privilege and a pleasure to do his work and to be worked at in it by him. A great experience, you know . . . Golden days!

Katie Mitchell

In 2001 Katie Mitchell directed Mountain Language *and* Ashes to Ashes *at the Royal Court in London.*

You say you're a Beckett director who's now turned to Pinter, feeling that there's a similarity between the two. What do you think the relationship is?

They lack sentimentality. In fact, abhor it, both writers, which means that there's a rigour, and a bleakness, which they share.

And what demands does that place on you as a director?

Actors resist going to places that those two writers ask them to go to, psychologically, and they will try to squirm off the hook of the character, so it's quite hard for me to coax them into the skin of the characters, because often it's a very dark place. *Endgame*, for example, is about the horror of separation, and we all live with that, but you don't want to spend much time in that zone. *Ashes to Ashes* on one level is a study of a breakdown of a marriage and we all fear that.

So that's something that they share.

Hmm, and irony and wit.

Can you give an example of these features working in performance?

Think of the pen sequence in *Ashes to Ashes*. She starts off with: 'Well, I put my pen on that little coffee table and it rolled off.' He immediately plays very light, and she says, 'It rolled right off, onto the carpet. In front of my eyes,' and he says, 'Good God!' At that point, he's just playing along; and then suddenly she comes in sideways by saying something else: 'This pen, this perfectly innocent pen.' And he replies, 'You can't know it was innocent.' He's still playing in a light word-play zone, but actually he's cutting under because he's starting to use the pen as a vehicle to get to *her* about the lover. So the pen becomes *her*. When she says, 'Why not?' she is still playing innocent. But then he says, 'Because you don't know where it had been. You don't know how many other hands have held it, how many other hands have written with it, what other people have been doing with it. You know nothing of its history.'

It's an exquisite piece of writing, but it's about a marriage breaking down. There was a tendency – because there were lots of other signs and signals in the text – to lighten it, as if the couple were playing a game as opposed to actually dealing with separating. They have the skin of the subject, the pen, to protect each other from what they're really transacting, which is: the man's really saying, 'How dare you betray me?' and the woman is trying to soften and lighten the betrayal, because it's not about betrayal. It's about these other things that are starting to stir and alter.

Does that make sense to you? It's a very delicate play because Pinter asks the character of Devlin to play 'No! Good God!' and then 'You can't know who's innocent,' so the character has to stay very firmly rooted in 'I've been betrayed'. This is a seventeen-to-twenty-year-old marriage, and suddenly there's infidelity – bang! – between them. It's quite hard because Pinter asks for very athletic manoeuvres from the actor.

How much comedy do you think there is in Ashes to Ashes*? Would you like to say something about the use of levity?*

A parallel would be the dog sequence in *Endgame*; he's made the dog with only three legs, and he hasn't put its sex there, and all of that. You can play just the levity of that between the two of them, you can play to the audience, to get everyone to laugh, but it should be played much more darkly and much more cruelly for the comedy to really work.

In life, every relationship has its habits and its patterns. Pinter is immaculate at constructing those patterns, so that we can sit there and recognise ourselves. When we're frightened, we can use wit to try and get the person who's frightening us out of the place where they're frightening us. Wit, irony can be a tool people use in relationships, but it certainly isn't the dominant tool in the transaction between that married couple. I'm sure you could play it all very, very lightly, but I think you'd run aground later, when people are drowning in the sea in Dorset.

Pinter writes fantastically accurately psychologically. I don't think his writing is abstract. I think a lot of people think it's abstract and nothing to do with real life. There's that something called 'Pinter acting' or 'Pinter pauses' or 'Pinter silences'. I don't know what that means. His characters are just human beings.

Pinter has been very resistant to actors' questions about the history of individual characters and the prehistory of the play. Do you have a view on Pinter's relationship to Stanislavskian acting?

Well, Stanislavsky does fascinate me, and I must say that I think his system is the best. We don't see much of it in this country because we are influenced by lots of other schools. In this production of *Ashes to Ashes* I had an actress who was trained at Drama Centre which is *the* Stanislavsky school in this country. And then alongside her I had someone who is instinctively a Stanislavsky actor but hasn't been trained and was slightly intimidated to begin with. So we started with character, back history, circumstances of the marriage, and using a factual analysis of the play, we constructed the back history. And we did improvisations, what their days had been like, other stages in their marriage, and we talked a lot about the fact that they had no children. And when I was talking with Harold, I think yes, to some extent, he does resist that way of thinking, but if it's going to lead the actor to making his play work, then I think he doesn't resist it.

So I did ask Pinter questions – How long have they been married? What university is he an academic at? – and he did give me answers. I'd always seen it as Oxford. He said, 'I think they've been married for about twenty, seventeen years,' and I said, 'Is there any infidelity going on?' 'No, no.' So he did answer quite a few of those questions, but they were asked over several meetings. I didn't go in with a long list. But then I did ask him a question which was key: 'Why don't they have children?' – a couple in their forties, that sort of couple. It's strange, it's curious.

He did defend that: 'Well, they always say about people who have no children that they have themselves, they have each other.' So I suppose he was slightly less direct in his answer of that question.

What do you think of Pinter's portrayals of women?

Well, I think he's capable of extraordinary lyricism, and he does write about female characters with great perception, and sympathy. It's a mistake not to see that as being part of the man. In the two plays that I directed, *Mountain Language* and *Ashes to Ashes*, I was fascinated that he put the emotional heart, and therefore the idea of the play, into the female characters, not the male. I'm reading *War and Peace* at the moment again – and Tolstoy puts the heart into Pierre and André, so the idea of the book is contained in those characters, not in the women, who are satellites. They act as foils to provoke and deepen our understanding of the men, whereas in these two Pinter plays, the men act as foils to the women, so it's the women we seek to understand. There are strong political ideas contained in these plays – and they are carried by women, not by men. It's like *Hamlet* from Ophelia's point of view – it's a fascinating choice.

I remember when we were trying to come up with the image for the two shows – a binding image – I brought in these photographs by a young American who killed herself when she was twenty-three, twenty-four, called Francesca Woodman. Pinter was absolutely drawn to these very strong, feminist and really extraordinarily beautiful photographs. And that was it, we decided that the binding image should be of a woman running through space.

It's quite rare, particularly if you're me and you do a lot of classical work, that the idea is located with the woman as opposed to with the man.

How do you relate that to The Homecoming, *for which Pinter has been criticised for producing a female character who is defined in relation to men – which is precisely the inverse of what you were saying?*

I don't know it intimately enough. I think that there is quite a male gaze on that woman. I'm not sure ultimately that I believe it, whereas I do believe other characters. I do believe their responses and reflexes; but it is a very contentious point, as of course is the line in *Mountain Language*, spoken by the man, who's trying all he can to intimidate and humiliate the women: 'intellectual arses are the best.' In 1990, that was contested by lots of feminists, who said that Pinter had crossed a line.

So how did you approach 'intellectual arses are the best'?

Well, I began by asking the actors to come up with examples of where they had been oppressed, or oppressed other people. There were a lot of domestic examples. Oppression can occur in a minuscule form in a relationship. You can oppress someone by not putting the rubbish out. It becomes an oppression over time. Or you are oppressed because your father doesn't allow you to do something that you want to do. So we started with very real things, that were near to the performers, and then moved further and further into exploring occasions when the state oppressed you, like when you got a parking ticket.

Then we moved into gender politics, which is more complicated. We talked a lot about sexual intimidation, so by the time we got to do the play, we'd looked at a whole range of different, small, concrete examples of oppression. So what happens in the play became only one tool used by that specific sergeant, in that prison at that moment, in order to demolish the voice of that woman. She keeps coming back, so finally they use very crude tools. The officers use much more sophisticated, intellectual tools. You see it straightaway: she's bright, quick, so he comes in with: 'Who? Who has been bitten . . . What is your name?' He's using head tools all the time to oppress her, to stop her making a complaint. That fails, so then he uses sledgehammer sexism, which does silence her.

You're unusual in that you prefer the later Pinter. What do you like about it?

Political conviction, isn't it? This is a man who has real convictions, unmoveable convictions about certain things. I just love *One for the Road, Precisely, Party Time* – all of those plays which are directly looking at political issues.

What are these political convictions then, from your point of view?

In *Mountain Language*, Pinter believes that it is fundamentally wrong that the Kurds shouldn't be allowed to speak their own language. And he believes that there are equivalent although smaller forms of oppression here, such as that he can write a poem about the bombing of Iraq, but he can't get it published. A year and a half ago I did Euripides, and I felt there was a similar sort of toughness – they're both hard-nosed political writers. Also, to be near someone who has those ideas is fantastically reassuring. Everything else is slightly slipping and slidy and ambivalent, and he writes plays which directly express his convictions. And he takes no prisoners.

And you don't see that level of conviction in the earlier plays?

I suppose the earlier plays deal a lot with domestic politics – the politics in relationships. I mean, *The Caretaker* is political: two brothers who can only communicate through a tramp and all three of them oppress and use and abuse each other. It's more about the politics with a small 'p' between people, but that's as dangerous as big, global oppression, in its way.

What do you admire about him as an actor?

He doesn't cheat. He doesn't fake. He plays it for real, and he plays it dangerously, he can go very close to the wire with his fellow actors.

And what is the wire?

Abuse.

Abusing the actors?

No, no, no. What I mean is, that as an actor you can play lots of different actions on a line. On any one line you can play a whole range of different types of action. And I think that he'll play the darker, harder choices. He's committed, and he's forceful. He tends to take the more forceful option, and the effect can be emasculating. Harold can play very light, delicate choices, but he can also put his whole body and psychology into delivering something hard; he has the strength as an actor to play very sharp, cruel actions.

There are two types of actors generally. There are those who play the audience as the main relationship and there are those who play the other character as the main relationship. There are some actors who are fantastically skilled, who always play the main relationship with the audience. Harold isn't like that. You could say (but not to him, of course!) that he's a great Stanislavsky actor, a great *interactive* actor, although for him it's just instinctive.

One more thing about Pinter as an actor. What would you like to direct him as?

I don't know. I'd be too frightened to direct him. But he might do King Lear . . .

Douglas Hodge

---

*Douglas Hodge's first Pinter role was in 1992, when he played
Foster alongside Pinter's Hirst in* No Man's Land. *Then in
1993 he created the part of Jake in* Moonlight. *In 1998 he
again acted alongside Pinter in* The Collection, *in a double
bill with* The Lover. *Later in the same year, he played the part
of Jerry in* Betrayal. *In 2000 he appeared as Aston in a revival
of* The Caretaker.

Tell me about your approach to acting in Pinter.

Well, firstly I would say that my approach to his work is
organic rather than academic. I feel he has this untram-
melled access to his subconscious that no other writer that I
know has. But also, his ear is exact. And his characters' inability to communicate deep emotion, and their construction
of smoke screens instead, is incredibly familiar to me.

What I've found in the fifteen or so Pinter plays I've acted in,
is that you have to get yourself into a really, *really* extreme
state of emotion before you go onstage. You have to be at a
pitch of tears, really, or of very intense violence or anger,
almost sort of psychotic. And then you have to behave as
politely as you possibly can. And that's all there is to it.

When you're onstage, you speak your lines as politely as
possible, and you try not to let that lid off. But the work that
you have to do before you go on gets you into an incredible
state of turmoil and a pitch of energy – like being in a com-
pression chamber. Really, you have to find the reason why
you are ready to kill the person next to you, or the great

bitterness that you have in your own life about who you're not. Or the enormous love that you're feeling for someone else, or the damage that's being done to you. Then you have to walk onstage, absolutely brimful of emotion and tears, and say, quietly, something simple like: 'Sit down.'

Can you tell me how that works in rehearsal?

In *Moonlight*, there are two sons who can't speak normally, who are just using old jokes and games, desperately trying to get to say that they love each other – or that they love their father – or that they hate him. They're desperately trying to speak to each other and to their mother or their father, and unable to do so. In rehearsal, sometimes you have to just let the lid off: you scream and rant, and let it be as messy as you feel it should be. But then you find that the catharsis is just too early: it can't come out in the play, the character just isn't capable of that, and it doesn't ring true. Actually, it's much more potent theatrically if the lid is kept on all the time.

But you do have to find these things in yourself, all the same. When I did *No Man's Land* with Harold and Paul Eddington, I really struggled with the last third of the play. We rehearsed it and rehearsed it and rehearsed it, and I was very struck that Paul never asked any questions. A lot of actors, younger actors, tend to want to analyse every single moment, and I'm a bit like that, whereas Paul would just get on with it, and Harold was the same. But in some ways it's the most ambiguous of Harold's plays, the hardest plot to work out. And halfway through rehearsals I found myself saying: 'Look, I'm going to have to come clean: I don't know what this is about! I have no idea what this means!' And there was this awful silence, and David Leveaux, the director, said, 'Well, what do you think it means?'

I felt very apologetic. I said, 'Look, I know that if we discuss this, it will diminish the poetic reverberation, the possibilities of what it could mean. But as an actor I need to make a specific choice. There's no point in me going on nebulously, playing it for ambiguity, because it won't mean one thing or the other. I have to decide what it means, and just play exactly what I believe is the truth, and then the audience can take that or leave it.'

So I talked with Harold. I told him the storyline that I had for myself, and Harold just said, 'Well, you know, as the writer, that's okay by me!' And we never discussed it again. I played my own story, and once I'd stopped attempting to portray some sort of ambiguity, I found I could just act, simply, like they could.

I suppose what you try and do as an actor is to make it so that the only words you can possibly utter within a certain situation are the ones that you're given. If you've done enough homework and enough thought and you're in the right place emotionally and physically, when somebody asks you that question onstage it's *impossible* for you to answer with any words but the ones you have in the script.

So do you think there is a special technique to acting Pinter?

People who've never played Pinter before spend an enormous amount of time finding their voice or finding the rhythm of it or trying to make it their own. Whereas the more you do it, the more you find you can access that mode naturally. You have to uncover the structure of the piece for yourself, but after that it's really best to keep it simple. You only have to try to play Harold's work with no pauses at all, and you find that it's false to answer so quickly. You can't actually say some things quickly, because there are too many things going on. The pauses will start to bash their way in. And, if there was a pause that felt false, Harold would be the first to say, 'That pause isn't true, forget it, cut it, don't have it! It's just there because when I wrote it I thought it would take time for him to go " . . . Yes!" Whereas if you can just go "Yes!" and that's just as potent, then just do it! It doesn't matter any more.' I mean, there is a slight straitjacket playing Pinter, there's no doubt about it. But not as much of a straitjacket, say, as playing Ayckbourn. If you do Ayckbourn, you're taught very quickly by the audience that there's one way to say it, and when you say it, they *rock*! It's incredible! And in spite of all your instincts to darken it and deepen it, if you just change the rhythm around a bit, you won't get a laugh and it doesn't work. The story isn't told – there's just no point in getting in the way of the writer's instinct for how it should come over.

And what you find with Pinter is that his instinct is fantastic. The plays work in a very traditional way, the form works. The tradition that he's inherited is invisibly there all the time. It's not as experimental as many people say. When I was doing *Betrayal* with Trevor Nunn I remember having a long conversation with him in which he insisted that the writer Pinter was closest to was Strindberg – and I was just indignant about this! I said, 'No, it's Noël Coward, surely!'

Coward loved Pinter's work. I wonder if you could tell me what similarities you see between the two.

Well, having played Strindberg and Coward, I know which tradition I'm linking into. There are striking similarities in the experience of performing Coward and Pinter. Because Pinter's got an ear for comedy, and at the same time an ear for old-fashioned, proscenium-arch, stand-up Noël Coward drama. He has an incredible theatrical sense of both comic and dramatic timing, like Noël Coward and the Marx Brothers combined!

I've done Pinter in theatres like the Almeida, sort of experimental, Peter Brookian open spaces, and then gone on to the West End, and I've found that the plays just work better in the old-fashioned proscenium-arch theatre. And when you're on tour and you go somewhere like the Bath Theatre Royal, suddenly Pinter characters come on and speak little platitudes to each other while being ready to murder each other at the same time, and you can never predict how the audience is going to respond.

Sometimes, one tends to be a little bit suspicious nowadays with so much laughter for Harold's work. You rehearse and rehearse, and you get into this bitter, sour world, and then it astonishes you the laughs you get when you get into the theatre! But there are moments on some nights where it's almost unstoppable, and you just have to go with it and ride the waves. And that's a wonderful experience.

But there can be another night, when the play's as potent, when there's utter silence, and you come off and say, 'We didn't do anything different then!' And yet you could hear a pin drop the whole evening. Either way, I think it's always wrong to allow those stormy, dark surges of feeling to eclipse the 'comedy of manners' aspect.

When I did *The Lover*, we looked at previous productions, photographs and so on, and there were so many strange 'experimental' versions. In Japan they were naked throughout the whole thing. And in France they were two men. But we also watched the original film of *The Lover*, and I thought that was just fantastic – so intelligently done! It was played as this incredibly clipped play of manners. Again, very Coward, really! Vivien Merchant was terribly sexy in it but still absolutely in keeping with the manners of the time. It was incredibly prim, really – but very quick, too. One thing I really noticed watching it is how slow the playing of Pinter has become these days, as people give you the importance of each line.

How do you see Pinter being performed in the future?

I think we will probably see productions of Pinter in the future which are really, really emotional and open; productions with screaming, shouting, violence: full of sound and fury, and deeply moving and emotional and prize-winning. But none of them will have the kind of choices that *he* would prefer or would have made, where you keep all that underneath and you just say the slightest thing and those words detonate much more effectively.

You have to remember Harold is a master of maintaining finesse and etiquette. But that's something that could change violently at any moment. He once said to me, 'I can take off my glasses faster than anyone.'

You mentioned doing Betrayal *with Trevor Nunn at the National. You played Jerry. Can you tell me a bit about that experience.*

It's by far my favourite play of his. I think its simplicity is sublime, and I think also it dramatises memory in a brilliant though simple way. One of the big problems I have playing roles I'm given as an actor is that when in real life someone gives you bad information, does something that makes you angry or upsets you, I personally don't really react there and then. I tend to react about a week later or in the car on the way home – *then* I have a massive argument with the person. And I think that's what most people do.

And I also think that five years later, faultlines can occur just through her doing something one day that you cannot forgive, though it only really becomes a faultline five years later. Sometimes relationships can be irreparably damaged by things that only cause them to break much, much later.

And the one thing that's *always* thwarted me as an actor is that onstage you *immediately* respond to the situations that you're in. Because all dramatists have to make you get angry or upset at the news that you receive there and then. And that has forever felt false to me.

Then I finally hit *Betrayal*, where someone had found a way where you could honestly respond to something that was said to you five years ago in a scene, five years later, with all that true, embittered, hopeless, desperate emotion! And the audience understood! The structure of *Betrayal* is such a simple and effective dramatic technique, but it also really dramatises memory. It dramatises the real nature of emotion, I think; happening and simmering and finally boiling over much later.

Betrayal shows how the smallest ticks and the tiniest habits and the little moments of exhaustion that people have, all become explained and revealed in the most fabulous way five years later. It's also sexy, funny and familiar.

You played Aston in The Caretaker, *with Gambon as Davies and Rupert Graves as Mick. Did you talk to Rupert about what the relationship was between the two brothers?*

I suppose the early chats we had were about what it used to be like before the operation; that I was the elder brother and how much verbal wit I had. In a way, I think that Mick and Aston had the ability of the two brothers in *Moonlight* with words . . . And then the operation changes everything, and one ends up looking after the other.

I reviewed that production in the press. I remember saying that you and Rupert were very moving at that point near the end after Mick smashes the Buddha. Aston enters and the text says that they look at each other and smile.

I remember we were in rehearsals, and I said to Harold, 'What did that mean, then, Harold? – What does it mean at the end there?' and he said, 'Well, he's – he's pleased to see him.' And I felt, 'Thank God!' It was so helpful.

It's the end of a long process. At the start Harold's got a grotty old room, he's got a tramp, and he's got a kind of real

[205]

guy, who maybe is a bit subnormal. He's got his brother who's got a van. And there's a kind of power play. So he starts imagining what they'd say to each other, once Aston's invited this tramp back. Now, the tramp gets the power, assumes pride of place. And Harold writes all this, and he's assuming at first that there will be a big fight in the end, you know – the tramp may be stabbed by one of the guys, because he's tried to take over, or the tramp may kill *them* or something. You can imagine him writing and thinking: 'It's going to be a great successful West End play, this . . . ' But incredibly – not incredibly, but wonderfully – Harold's integrity won't let him do anything dishonest. And given the characters are who they are, he can't get any of them to kill each other, and none of them will do anything that'll really sell out seats in the West End! They will just speak to each other. Yet somehow it works. As it says in *The Birthday Party*, 'They just talk.'

What was it like doing The Collection *with Pinter acting alongside you? You as the jealous husband James, and him as the jealous older gay man?*

Great! The interesting thing was that he was there immediately. He needed no rehearsal. He knew exactly who the man was, had an image of him, could see him very clearly, knew exactly what he'd intended and knew the rhythm of the lines. He was very funny and did the 'slum-slug' speech unbelievably well. Of course, he knows those kind of old poofs very, very well, you know!

I imagine he might possibly have encountered a few in his time in the theatre . . . ?

One or two, possibly.

Harry Burton

Harry Burton has played Jerry in Betrayal, *Fred in* Moonlight
*(the BBC Radio production in which Pinter played Andy), and
created the part of Jimmy in* Party Time, *which was also made
as a Channel Four film. The part of Jimmy consists of one long
speech on the experience and effects of torture.*

I saw you as Jimmy in Party Time, *and we've just watched the
film together. It's a harrowing and extraordinary speech. What do
you remember of the demands and the rewards of that role?*

When we did *Party Time*, the Gulf War was not long past,
and there were two airmen who were captured and held.
And I remember reading the account by one of them of what
it was like to be incarcerated. And it was as if Harold had
been on the inside of it. This guy said that actually the most
frightening thing of all was to hear what was happening to
other people. Not least, of course, because it meant that you
might be next, or that they were working towards you, but
in other ways, too. Which I think reveals something which
Harold understands at a very deep level as a man and as a
writer: that one's connection to other human beings is paramount, and that when death is close, when violent and awful
death is upon you, what brings that home is the suffering of
your fellow creature. In some extraordinary way, Harold
had the essence of this experience, and turned it into this –
into this poem.

What was it like having Pinter as director?

Well, he was extremely helpful. I certainly don't think up to that point as an actor that I'd been required to do anything comparable. For one thing, my entrance was into a doorway framed with light, so that the minute the door opened at all, this extremely bright chink of light would appear, which would then become wider, and then a whole doorway of light as it opened. For me this meant that I was in a box, representing a doorway, and the three walls inside the box were extremely high-wattage strip lighting.

How to step out of that oppressive box into the play and deliver this speech was a process that he really guided me through. All I remember really about it was that he just encouraged me very gently to take out any inflection, just to – just take away anything that even *suggested* an intellectual observation on what he was saying. You see, the way it works is that it's already happened. It's just that he's still living it internally, living in the horror, perpetually.

Did he talk to you in those terms?

I don't think he did, no. I think he said, 'Jimmy is a ghost.' We came to the conclusion that the way to play it as an actor was from the point of view of somebody who was talking about having died. It's almost impossible to describe. You play it in the end by not playing it.

As an actor, and in terms of a rehearsal process, you've got to let go of an awful lot of baggage – it's amazing. It's a two-and-a-half minute speech, and it took three weeks of rehearsal to take away the complications.

Harold kept asking me just to let go more, just let go *more*, and just let go *more*. To the point where, you know, it was possible for it to be real, not dramatised. And if the girl playing the girl has done her job, then every time his name's mentioned – 'What's happened to my brother Jimmy?' – that has a cumulative impact. So when Jimmy arrives he doesn't have to come on and do a tap dance. The words do the whole damn thing. It took tremendous physical stillness and depth of breathing. Which Harold taught me. He gave that to me as a discipline.

By direct technical input, or going for the effect and getting you to generate that?

He doesn't direct, I don't think, by technical observation. Although, of course, he's very assured technically himself as an actor. As a director, he understands actors absolutely *par excellence*. As Jimmy, I had to make a tremendous effort every night to get into the right state of concentration. And it was an incredibly exacting thing to do. I mean, what Harold was asking of me as the actor was to be prepared to go into that bleak imaginative space and fully occupy it for the necessary time. And really I didn't have a particularly strong psychological make-up myself at the time – in fact I was all over the shop as a person. And there I was, under the stage at the Almeida, trying to detach myself from what I could hear above me, the rest of the cast talking to each other and getting laughs . . . it was hard, and Harold understood, I think, that it was hard.

And then when we got together for the film version nine months later, I remember him saying to me, you know, 'You've got to do it again.' And I said, 'Well, how many times?' And he said, 'I won't let you do it more than twice.' And I said, 'Okay, right, all right, I can cope with twice.' Because I had to go back to this place. It's a desolate spot in the psyche that you have to find and then be prepared to stay in, and let that come through you. And that's what Harold gave me, certainly with that play – a real, extraordinary object lesson in how to let something come through you rather than you be the energy. Let the energy come from elsewhere, you just make yourself available for it – by whatever means necessary.

You were in Moonlight, *this time with Pinter as a fellow actor. How was that?*

I never spoke to him in the play, because the boys don't speak to their father, but having him in the company was a joy. Because he was nervous and a bit jumpy, and Doug [Hodge] and I were winding him up and in the studio we were giving him a bit of chat. The studio at Maida Vale was on split levels, and he and Sara Kestelman were on the top level and we were below being the kids, as it were, in the basement, me and Indira [Varma] and Douglas. And a couple of times he barked downstairs, you know, 'Shut bloody up, will you!' 'Cause he was, you know, trying to – trying to get a line right or something. But he revelled in it. He revelled in it. And he was very gracious in letting someone else direct it.

Actor to actor, what do you admire?

He has a sort of mercurial energy as an actor, which is just wonderful to behold, because it's a different – quite a different facility from his gravitas facility, even his grand old man facility, his umpiring facility, whatever it is. As an actor he has access to this tremendously youthful energy. Even as Andy, playing a man who's dying. Andy's still funny, still talking about his sexual conquests, getting almost sweaty about lesbianism and all that, and Harold brought that out brilliantly.

That's what you want from actors: a limitless pool of some kind of high-octane, spirited energy that can be honed and disciplined so that it can take the actor where the story needs the actor to go. And Harold has that high-octane stuff – in petrol-station loads!

Over the years, on top of whatever he was born with as a pugilist, he has perhaps involuntarily, but by necessity, had to develop an extremely thick outer shell. But all that goes when he's acting, I think. He just becomes playful. It reminds me of *The Dwarfs*, which I really like, because it's full of that spirit. It has these young men who are full of it though they don't know how to hone it or discipline it.

Moving on to Betrayal, *what was it like to play Jerry?*

Playing Jerry was probably the hardest thing I've ever done. Because the play's like a piece of music. I think Peter Hall said it was like Mozart. Well, I'm unusual among actors because I've played several Mozart operas and acted Figaro, Leperello and Papegeno, and Jerry requires a lot of the same sense of the overall music of the piece.

Critics and actors often say, 'Oh, it's a musical score' and to me that's usually little more than claiming prestige for the person who's saying it, and even an excuse for mystification – pretending that you don't need to know what's going on and work hard to realise what people mean in Pinter. Are you saying it's a similar experience practically?

If you were, for example, a singer in an opera, you would learn your part but then your part actually is meaningless, out of context. You have to know the whole composition, and when the conductor gives you your cue you not only have to sing, but sing in a way that really fits with the structure and the nuances of the performance as a whole. *Betrayal* is riddled with silences and pauses, and what I found doing Jerry was that you'd only done half your job in preparation once you'd learnt your part. I then had to learn the pauses and the silences, so that one could *play* them. And, you know, just as a piece of music requires diminuendos and silences and pauses and so on, every silence, every pause has a value musically, and if you don't play them, you're not hearing the piece – you're not playing the *notes* properly either.

I think that what you say about Betrayal *is undeniable. The danger, of course, when you play drama as chamber music is that*

*it becomes studied, even stilted. How, as an actor, do you guard
against that?*

You have to catch the quality of the energy that's underneath the music.

*Can you say something about Jerry as a person, where he's com-
ing from and what his energy is . . . ?*

I don't know where to start, but I mean, he's charming, he's
immature, he's greedy, he's bright but extremely unconscious in some areas of his life. He's ambitious. He's obviously a serial liar and betrayer. You know, one thinks of Oscar
Wilde saying that men destroy the thing they love most. I
mean, somewhere Harold says *Betrayal* is a play about ten
years in the friendship of two men. And Jerry's *cri de coeur*
when he realises that he's been caught red-handed but that
his friend has not let on that he knew, is 'But you were my
best friend!' That's Jerry's ability to deflect from himself
onto Robert the seriousness of the crime. Jerry basically
accuses Robert of a worse betrayal than his own, than the
sexual infidelity.

Apart from anything else, the play tracks the progression of
Jerry, which is a sort of progression I identify strongly with
– as a man – of the painful acquisition of consciousness,
through – through the means that the soul and the divine
create for one.

*In the sense that there are forces beyond them? You're not really
invoking supernatural forces or suggesting that the play is about
the soul and the divine?*

I *am* invoking – well, I am invoking *archetypal* forces, as I
would call them. In other words, forces which are not human
but which are in the ground beneath our feet and in our very
essence as individuals. There is a terrific energy in Jerry – as

there is in Harold. It's people like Harold, and people like me, and probably people like you, who are lucky enough to have that energy in their bodies, and who then find that it gets them into the most awful trouble!

Now, you've given what to me seems quite a dark and critical reading of Jerry so far: ambitious, dynamic, greedy, deceitful, when in many ways he seems to me the most naive and transparent member of the trio. Despite being the principal male deceiver in the basic triangle, he's by far the most emotionally direct, idealistic and naive, surely?

Well, it's that naivety that's so dangerous. It's that naivety that burns houses down with children and women in it, you know, if you're a man! It's precisely that naivety. Psychologically what you're describing, and what you're dealing with, with Jerry, is a tremendously large ego.

Something's come up, which is that you've spoken of Jerry as a mixture of a kind of greedy, open-hearted, almost innocent optimism. If he's greedy then it's in an open, optimistic way that wants to share and give at the same time, like a child or a baby. And it reminds me of the generous, greedy, childlike energy that you've just described Pinter as having. Pinter's love of life is omnivorous, or at least it includes anything that isn't selfish, or cruel, I think – certainly he's a very open-hearted man who believes the best of others and loves his friends. And it's a cliché, of course, but Jerry is to some extent Pinter. Did you think about that when you were playing it?

Well, I've known Joan Bakewell since I was a child, grew up with the Bakewells, and Harold's very open about how the play includes a lot of things that they did, Joan, Michael and Harold, and of course I thought about that. But to me what is very interesting, I think, is that in the darkened bedroom at the end of *Betrayal* you have a direct parallel to the myth of Cupid and Psyche, where Cupid marries Psyche, but she mustn't see that he's a god. So he keeps her in darkness, and they enter this state of erotic bliss, and she becomes accustomed to being made love to and seduced in this fantastic erotic heaven. I think it's an example of how Harold's work is finely tuned to a certain kind of mythological level of – of imagery, probably unconscious. But it is so erotic, that moment in that bedroom. And the stakes are so high. And then her husband comes in, and he immediately starts lying to his best friend, saying, 'I decided to take this opportunity to tell your wife how beautiful she was.' And he says, 'Quite right.' And he compounds this terrible thing, Jerry, by saying – by saying furthermore, you know, 'I speak as your oldest friend. Your best man.' And Robert seems to be saying, be my guest.

On the same lines, did you think that, as Jerry, you were pushing Emma towards Casey? From your face it doesn't look like you did!

In the end it doesn't work for actors to go too deep into conjecture of what motivates people – I mean, it's just what fucking happens! We did talk about Casey, and the fact that at one point Jerry turns up at Robert and Emma's house and she says, 'What are you doing here?' and he says, 'I was having tea with Casey.' And she says, 'Where?' And Jerry says, 'He's left Susannah. He's living alone round the corner.' And Emma says, 'Oh.' It registers with her that Casey's now living round the corner, and he's separated from his wife. Now, at that point we all looked at one another and said, 'Hang on, you know, what is she doing? Planning the next betrayal of her husband?' And of course you can't *play* that! You can't *play* that she's writing down in a little notebook, 'Must fuck Casey next week. Marvellous chance. Marvellous opportunity.' But there it is in the script.

In other words, I suppose again my experience of *Betrayal* was as a process of elimination. You see, finally playing *Betrayal* is nothing to do with naturalism at all. Because if it was naturalism, then every night you could play one line in one way because it feels natural, and the next night you play it in a different way because *that* feels natural. But that's no good. Because you've got to play it in the right way so that you connect to the next line and the one before. So as an actor you can't be naturalistic at all in the way you approach it.

Even though you have to give everything to make it real?

Quite. It has to be real, but it's like you can't suddenly, in the middle of a Schubert quintet, play as if it was Gershwin. What you're trying to arrive at – as actors and as an ensemble, as your little orchestra – is an agreement about how you can best honour the piece. If you look at it all the time from that perspective, then you finally do inexorably come to the core of the writing. And when you hit it, you know it.

Can you think of a scene in Betrayal *where it was hard to find the way to play it, or one where you struggled to agree?*

I think that the first scene in *Betrayal* is particularly difficult, because it begins with an exchange of apparently extremely commonplace, mundane, apparently 'ordinary' stuttering comments. It's an almost embarrassed reunion between two people who have had an affair but who haven't seen each other for two years. To find the right way to play Jerry in that scene was the single hardest thing for me in the rehearsal period, because again and again I would be losing concentration. Again and again I would kind of just slightly drift off the line, because of all the options and possible inflections – the rise and fall of the voice, the pitch of a question, the hint of anger, the suggestion of humour. There are all these infinite variations in how you would play a particular line. Actors succeed or fail by their ability to retain the memory of what does and doesn't honour the writing. In the first scene of *Betrayal* there's a lot of tension and a lot to remember, and to keep out of that scene. It's like landing an aircraft on instruments only, you just have to trust the writing. And it just requires tremendous concentration.

What parts in Pinter do you want to play next?

Well, I'd like to play Foster in *No Man's Land* but Harold says I'm too old. What I like about Foster is that, like the waiter in *Celebration*, he has this interesting kind of febrile imaginative quality – almost as if I could say anything and it would be true, just because I've imagined it. And whether his grandfather did know all these people in *Celebration*, or whether Foster did, you know, carry a gun and have all these experiences in the East, is secondary to the fact of *imagining* it, playing with tall stories and funny voices and turns of phrase like an actor.

You see, my own little theory when I saw *Celebration* was that if Jimmy in *Party Time* was dead, then he's come back to life again, and the girl in *Moonlight* is speaking after death. And I think something has happened in the last ten years for Harold, and some aspect of himself that was dead is now well and truly alive. And it's alive in the waiter in *Celebration*. It's that playfulness. These people are now alive!

I mean, Harold's a lucky fucker. He has that gift, that ability to go down into his unconscious nature, by birth. The rest of us have to, you know, fight tooth and claw for it. Imagine how painful it was for Harold when he lost it, in the years when he couldn't write those plays. And perhaps – and maybe he wouldn't disagree – it may have had something to do with that thing of taking credit for what is mysterious, you know, for what is divine in origin. You know, hubris. And what the gods give, they also take away. The minute human beings start forgetting that they're in a process and that they're lucky to be participating, and start saying, 'Well, *I* originate this, this is what *I* do, and you can all go fuck yourselves,' they just take your toys away, those gods!

My favourite image that Harold ever described to me was this moment in his teenage years, in his home kitchen with his mum and his dad. He said he was about seventeen. And they were just all in the kitchen. And quite suddenly his mother fainted. Just passed out. And the two men, or the young man and his father, stood there and the father turned to Harold and said, 'Look after your mother,' and then *he* fainted. Leaving Harold stood there with both his parents unconscious on the floor, on an ordinary normal day, you know.

Now, there's something in that image which I think, you know, is very important to who Harold is. I'm not saying that that moment changed everything. But there is such aloneness in that moment, demanding courage. And I think that's what you're dealing with, with Harold: courage and loneliness. And this innate gift to clear the channel for when the unconscious has information that he needs to bring into the world. You can feel the discipline, because of the incredible economy in the writing.

Sam Mendes

Sam Mendes directed The Birthday Party *at the National Theatre in 1995.*

When did you first come across Pinter's work?

I suppose it was at school. I think it was *The Caretaker*. And I remember reading great tracts of it out loud to myself in my bedroom: because one of the things you discover most swiftly about Harold's work is that it's designed to be spoken. And it lingers in the mind long after you've read it out loud, particularly as I was then a young schoolkid just beginning to get the sense that I might want to work in the theatre. I suppose I must have been a wannabe actor of some sort. That's long gone! But it does make you want to be an actor, reading Pinter. It does make you want to speak the lines.

And then I sat through numerous pretty poor productions of *The Caretaker* and *The Homecoming* at university, with the local nineteen-year-old star playing Davies, the usual thing.

But I think I approached it as literature initially, and found myself reading it out. That's how it first came into view. And when you read it, you remember it. Sometimes you find actors drying on words and syllables in Pinter plays because they know that they've got to get it just right. But aside from that pressure it's the easiest thing to remember in the world! I mean, we can all quote tens of lines of Pinter. It really is memorable. The only other thing that's that easy to remember is Shakespeare.

If you were to rekindle the desire to be an actor, which of Pinter's characters would you play and why?

In Pinter I think I'd like to play Goldberg in *The Birthday Party*. There are the Goldbergian roles, do you know what I mean? I suppose it's those parts that are the least emotionally engaged, and the most mysterious, as well. In actual fact, they have all now been rather brilliantly played by Harold himself, and they tend to be the most fun to play!

What do you mean, 'the least emotionally engaged'?

Well, I think they had to put themselves through the least during the course of the evening of drama. I don't think Goldberg goes through a huge emotional thing. I mean, he's not Stanley, neither is he Davies!

And his traumas are more verbalised.

Yeah, absolutely. He complains about being hot and sweaty and has palpitations at one point, loses his cool, but that's about as far as it goes!

But I think that it's an extraordinary feature of Harold's work that you, as an actor or a director, have to treat it almost like – well, now I sound pretentious – almost like directing opera. Because in opera you learn the music of the piece, and then you have to find the fuel that will take you on the emotional journey that takes you naturally to those places. You have to start with the music, learn the music, and then you have to find an emotional journey that takes you to the notes. And it's the same thing with Harold.

I mean, there is a music in the text: you have to find the music, and then you have to find what's going on under the surface. But it's very, very difficult to operate in reverse, it's very difficult to sit down and say, 'Well, where has this man come from, what is he doing?' So the conventional means by which you would normally direct plays are thrown out of the window.

There's a great story about Beckett directing *Waiting for Godot* at the Royal Court in '76. It was the Schiller production of *Waiting for Godot*, which he recreated in London. And the actors went almost insane. He rehearsed for ten weeks and he went line by line, he never ran anything, he simply went line by line. And he wouldn't stop until they had exactly the rhythm of the four, five lines, six lines, ten lines, twenty lines that he was looking at. And then he moved on. He moved on and he moved on. And he did this for eight weeks, and they never got to run anything. At the end of the eight weeks they ran it, and what they expected was a car crash and something utterly mechanical, but what happened was a performance of utter spontaneity and total freedom. And that's what it's like rehearsing Pinter. It's not all fun! Because you're absolutely – you're going line to line, and it takes a long time. But it pays off.

Can you think of a scene in The Birthday Party *to illustrate that?*

All of it! [*Laughs.*]

But in your production of The Birthday Party, *for instance, take Stanley's speech about Lower Edmonton and the concert he was supposed to give. Did you sit down with Anton Lesser, the actor, and discuss the extent to which you thought that story was true?*

Oh yes, absolutely. I think you have to discuss the secret play. Because in the end the actors must know what *they* mean. But I don't want the production to make that clear. The mystery of the play remains for the audience. I think in order to play it with any level of conviction, the actors have to make up their minds. And sometimes I will say to an actor, 'Listen, I just want *you* to know what you mean. I want you to know whether you're making it up or not.' And more often than not, the way to discover what is the appropriate answer to that is to say, 'Well, play it as if it didn't happen and now play it as if it did.' And in the case of Stanley I happen to think he believes it did. That's his version of events. But I think that an audience understands that something else was going on – that he is choosing to use this as an excuse for the life that he chose to live, as opposed to the life of a successful man.

But when the work is being played properly what the audience takes is different, case to case, audience member to audience member. Because it has resonance in all directions and therefore you're seeking *not* to be reductive about simple meaning.

What you're looking for is the perfect-shaped pebble that will send ripples as far out to the side of the pond as possible, be it in the reading of a line or a performance. This will leave all options open and yet something utterly concrete in the middle of it, in which every decision has been made and every choice is made on firm ground and foundations.

How are these foundations built with actors?

Obviously that involves a lot of questions and hard work. 'Where are they taking Stanley? And what's the relation between Goldberg and McCann?' And all of those things. But they're only a means to an end for the actors. You might say to Michael Gambon in rehearsal, 'Who is Davies, and where is he from? Where is he actually living? How long has he actually been there? Where does he really belong?' and all those things. And [*laughs*] he might quite justifiably say, 'I'm not going to tell you. I know, but I don't want *you* to know.' It's a question of whether the actor wants that kind of dialogue with the director. Either way is perfectly reasonable.

I certainly know that some directors would like not to have that question at all! But I certainly would, and feel that whatever can fuel a precise and clear signal to an audience from an actor is a good thing, do you see what I'm saying?

That phrase you used a minute ago, 'the secret play', it sounds like one you have used before.

Yeah, it is!

Specifically about Pinter, or about other playwrights?

Well, I mean, he would be a classic example. Because I think that in Harold's plays there is a network of previously existing relationships that are brought onto the stage. For example, the way in which Goldberg and McCann operate together, you need to feel that they're in tune, that they have been together for a certain time. So you and the actors sit down and go, 'Well, okay, let's work out how long, why, how, where they met and so on.' And you can come up with absolutely crazy ideas, it doesn't matter, as long as what you see on stage has a fluidity and an ease.

Now, you can get that on certain occasions without a single day's rehearsal. You can get that immediately. So it's not to say that it's absolutely essential, but with discussion you're more likely to get it and keep it. Because, of course, theatre is about repetition, not about inspiration, most of the time. Inspiration happens in rehearsals, but repetition is the key. Because you have to have enough of an outside eye to retain and remember everything that you've learned up to that point and repeat it, with varying degrees of difference, but nevertheless you have to repeat it. With Harold, the music has to remain absolutely concrete and intact, and rhythms that are set up in the fourth, fifth week of rehearsals have to then be basically controlled and repeated thereafter.

There is still an enormous amount of freedom within the structure. Line readings often are not the same, but the rhythms remain very, very similar.

And on structure I remember actually once having a conversation with Harold and Antonia Fraser. I think he was doing *Old Times,* and Antonia said, 'Oh, *Old Times* is my favourite play.' And I said to Harold, 'What's your favourite play of yours?' He said, 'Oh, *The Homecoming.*' And I said, 'Why?' and he said, 'Well, it's all a question of shape.' And I said, 'And what shape is *The Homecoming?*' and he said, 'Well, it's kind of *shhh-kkowww!* and that's it!' [*Makes Pinter's gesture, the flat right hand, fingers together and extended, rising to a peak and then making a sharp chopping descent.*]

Which of course you can't put on the page! So *The Homecoming*'s wedge-shaped! But it's the *shhh-kkowww* and that's it, you know! There's a purity of line and form that he strives for, a completeness that is best described by making a gesture with your hands and a noise, as opposed to any words, and you absolutely understand what he means. He's saying something has come out of the marble that just is a perfect shape, you know what I mean? Each character has a shape, each line has a shape, the words have shape. And without wanting to be too waffly about it, really, in the end it comes down to the fact that someone either hears the music of the line or they don't, and you can't instruct someone about a musical voice. It doesn't matter how good an actor they are, if they don't hear it, it's like not having an ear for music.

Can you help actors if they don't hear it?

All the actors I've worked with on Pinter have been superb actors. But if they don't have that kind of ear, it's very difficult. I heard of one actor who did *The Birthday Party,* but couldn't *hear* it, couldn't hear the music. He was a brilliant actor. But apparently he didn't hear the music and he lost a lot of the comedy. For instance, there are lines in the play, like where McCann says, 'You've always been a true Christian' and Goldberg says, 'In a way!' Now, you hear Harold say, 'In a way,' it's a great line. You give that line to Harold, it'd bring the house down. But you either hear it or you don't, you know! So the director was trying to explain the joke, and the actor was ringing Harold up and saying things like, 'So this – this Jewish thing, then, Harold: what is it? Hey, do you – do you know any Jews?' And Harold: 'Well, *I'm* Jewish, for example!' 'Are you? Well, could we talk about it?' Which left Harold a little bemused!

Talking of comedy, something I think comes over much better in performance than on the page is that he's a master of the running gag for a theatrical audience, don't you think?

Oh, definitely. He's *incredibly* funny! He's just one of the funniest writers. He has written many of the funniest lines and the funniest scenes in modern drama. I don't think he knows where it comes from, and if he does, he won't say.

Because – I'll say it again, put my cards on the table, you know: Peter Hall says that Pinter's early plays are too funny, too audience-directed. And I think what he wants Pinter's work to be is an austere, neo-Beckettian, opaque piece of semi-ethereal, high modernism.

Yeah! Incredible, the 'semi-ethereal, high modernism'!

I feel that that's less important to your own approach, which depends a great deal on comedy and a humorous rapport with the audience. Did you know that Pinter wanted Sid James to play Max in the first production of The Homecoming?

No, I didn't! But I can absolutely imagine him being brilliant. And of course, you long to see Max Wall play Davies . . . I would. I mean, those kind of figures are absolutely perfect for Harold's work. I mean, Max Wall was in *Waiting for Godot*, I believe, famously.

Oh, absolutely! He did Private View, *plenty of things, I think, later on.*

And Keaton, of course, for Beckett. There is this figure of the man in the bowler hat which haunts mid-twentieth-century literature, from the days of – and you can trace it through Bloom, through Orwell and *Down and Out in Paris and London* and into, obviously, Chaplin and Laurel and Hardy and Keaton. And there is this sense of the kind of dignity of the comedian and the great sad clown's eyes. I mean, that feeds straight into Davies, this sense of the wandering tramp. And it's –

What does the bowler hat do in that?

Well, I think it crosses over. I mean, Chaplin founded the great kind of iconic image for the man who was both chameleon and wanderer. And there is a sense of the root-lessness of the gypsy and the inspired invention and genius of the chameleon, combined. And that image flows through into *The Caretaker* in some way. I mean, I think that he is a great iconic twentieth-century figure.

Working on a play with Harold, the other thing that happens is that he does tell you, he's very straightforward about the genesis of his plays. And he tells you a handful of very short stories about how the play came to be, and the handful of short stories about *The Birthday Party* are about as clear an indication as to how you should do the play and what it means as you could possibly get. He talks about very concrete things when he talks about the genesis of his plays.

Being in stinking digs and so on . . . ?

Well, that he was – in wherever it is, Worthing, in *My Kingdom for a Horse*. And he bumps into this fellow in a bar, and asks, 'Do you know anywhere?' And he replies, 'Well, I do know somewhere, but I wouldn't recommend it – go and have a look for other places. If you can't find anything, I'll be back here at three o'clock.' And Harold looks, can't find anything. And he goes back, and sure enough there he is alone in the pub. And he goes up to him and he says, 'Look, I can't find anywhere else. What about this place?' So he takes him back, up the back streets, and there's this Victorian terraced house that we all know and love in English seaside towns. And he shares a room with this man for a week! Bedding on the floor. And there is this bizarre relationship between this lodger and this superannuated, sex-crazed landlady who clearly is obsessed with him, and in some kind of weird sexual game with him. Harold turns to him and says at one point, 'Why do you stay here?' And the bloke says, 'There's no-where else.' Which is one of the great lines! In the middle of Worthing or wherever it was. And that does appear in the play.

But in *The Birthday Party*, the deceptive thing is that the moral centre of the play is the person who speaks the least, which is Pete, Petey. And that was brought home to me by Trevor Peacock in the performance I directed. It was really an extraordinary performance.

What did he do and what did he play to make him the moral centre and to give him the right to say that great line at the end?

'Don't let them tell you what to do!' Another great line! Well, I mean, it was Trevor, really, in my production. It's a terrible world of loss underneath the surface, and an enormous well of emotion and sadness. And in him is the English inability to speak, the years of sitting on emotional traumas and never talking about them until it's too late. The paralysis of being English.

And then there's that whole world: the seaside town and all the people who live in a time-warp in those places.

I think it's very interesting the way that place is dealt with in Harold's work. Location is always key. You know there are those characters who talk about it, and those who talk about it generally speaking are weaving a fiction. You know, the piano recital, Goldberg's stories, 'We used to come here when we were kids' – the fictions that they tell.

It's a bizarre concoction. And Davies' endless invention in *The Caretaker* is this kind of web of words that start with infinite riches in a little room, which is what's going on in *The Caretaker* – these endless universes created by people who never open the door and never leave.

And then there are the people like Petey who do go outside but don't speak about it. They actually live in the world. And Petey puts the deckchairs out on the beach. It's not mentioned by him. Or he says he's going off to play chess. Almost nothing, but these things seem to be so well chosen and they seem to show someone who actually is engaged in contact with other human beings. And so when he says at the end, 'Don't let them tell you what to do,' you realise that he's the only human being onstage. So it's a shocking moment. Because you realise that he's seen everything. And he responds to it. I mean, in a way Petey, you know, kills Stanley because of what he tells Goldberg and McCann! But he tries to protect him, and that's terribly moving.

Would you like to say something about sexuality and the treatment of female characters in the plays?

Well, I think it's changed. I think it's developed as he's developed as a writer. I think you see a fear and an objectification of women in the early works. It's *brilliant* objectification, but I think that in *The Homecoming*, Ruth is a creature from another planet. And she feels like it, with immense power over men. And Meg in *The Birthday Party* is the opposite of that, so sexuality is either comic like her or it's frightening like Ruth. But, of course, as you go through the mid-period plays, like *Betrayal* and *Old Times*, these feature extremely deep figures who are the women. They're closer to the women, presumably, in Harold's own life. And then they become the central figures in the plays.

But I think the sexuality is omnipresent. What can I say about it? It shifts across the body of work, but it's always there. I mean, just go and see *One for the Road*, in which Harold's acting this week. The sexual weirdness is fantastically powerful! And it's not just heterosexual.

The fatal mistake with Harold's work is performing it as a hallowed text. I say this because I've just seen him do it. The best possible example of how to do it is with Harold himself. And I know it sounds stupid, but it's really very true; there is no question that he'll ever miss a gag! Even as the torturer in *One for the Road*, he says, 'Are you coming to love me? Ha ha ha — your wife is! We're very keen on her, let me tell you.' And it's extremely funny and utterly terrifying: it is the quintessence of Pinter. You're aware simultaneously that he is making a joke, and yet utterly intent on destruction.

The good thing about talking to practitioners and talking in practical terms about the play is that you're drawn to examples of when it works and why it works. And at that point in *One for the Road* it's intrinsically comic and yet all the more frightening for it.

And I think that that's why he went through such a long period of not writing plays at all: because when you don't question it, you don't question it when it's there, you don't question when it's *not* there. It just is. And then one day he says, 'Well, hang on a minute, I've just had . . . I've got something I want to write' and he writes *Moonlight* because he's sitting in a café in Brighton and he's just visiting his father, and he doesn't know why it's just bubbled up, and why he wrote half the play in a notebook sitting out looking at the sea. I mean, he just did.

And in fact in this day and age of describing what it is that you're going to do and doing it, going – 'I've got a movie and here's the studio, and I'm going to pitch the movie! This is what it's going to be, it's what you're going to feel, you're going to do this, and it's going to – this is going to happen and that's going to happen. There's going to be a big explosion but it'll be a happy ending,' you know! It's such a relief to find somebody who says, 'I don't know. I just don't know. I am an artist. And what will be, will be.' You know, and so in a way he's both the most wonderful and the most frustrating person to write a book about, which is perhaps why there are so many books about the Becketts of this world and the Pinters of this world.

He offers a myriad of possibilities but no answers. And I suppose I'm unwilling to be drawn into the answer-giving, because I don't have them. And I would only just be adding my voice to the throng of people who just guess, frankly.

I am proud and pleased that I know Pinter. And I'm really pleased that he's out there and that he's English. What about you?

Proud to have known him. He's the most influential English playwright of the postwar years by – by *miles*! Influential not just for playwriting but in all sorts of things, from comedy to television to films. Everything from Pete 'n' Dud to the Python stuff.

The man's also amazing. He's seventy years old, he's standing onstage round the corner, as we speak, performing *One for the Road*. I mean, the man is absolutely extraordinary! And he *cares*. May we all care enough when we are seventy years old to write letters to the newspaper about things that we believe in! It staggers me that he has that energy and that fire burning in him.

And the beauty of it is the relish he takes in it. I rang him after the first preview of *The Birthday Party* at the National, which had gone pretty well, and he rang me later at home and said, 'I'm absolutely thrilled that it's gone so well.' And I said, 'Look, Harold, you opened this play in 1958 and it closed in a week. Now it's at the National Theatre, a masterpiece, and how does it feel?' He said, 'Bloody good!'

The relish he still takes is a wonderful thing.

Acknowledgements

This book reproduces the following interviews from their respective sources:

HAROLD PINTER INTERVIEWS

Harry Thompson, *New Theatre Magazine*, II.2, January 1961
Lawrence M. Bensky, *The Paris Review*, 1966
Miriam Gross, *The Observer*, 5 October 1980
Anna Ford, *Omnibus/The Listener*, 27 October 1988
Mireia Aragay and Ramon Simo, Universitat de Barcelona,
    Departament de Filologia Anglesa i Alemanya,
    6 December 1996

PETER HALL INTERVIEW

Catherine Itzin and Simon Trussler, *Theatre Quarterly*,
    No. 16, 1974

*

I am grateful to all the interviewees in this book for giving their time and opinions so generously. If a little of the rigour, intelligence and warmth with which they approach and discuss Pinter's work comes through in the book then the process has been more than worthwhile.

The Hackney duo, Mick Goldstein and Henry Woolf, are dispersed to Sydney and Saskatoon, but remain indomitable in body and spirit. This book quotes only briefly from their many conversations with me, but its account of Pinter would have been impossible without them.

Many of my family and friends gave invaluable support to me in the process of compiling the final version. Extra thanks and love are due to Martin and Jonathan Smith, and to Rebecca Arnold.

Above all I must thank Harold Pinter, who has not only contributed the Foreword but has encouraged this project from its first existence as a twinkle in a publisher's eye. As a friend he is faithful, generous, and fiercely loyal, and even if discretion would allow it, there is far too little space here to do justice to his kindness to me. As an artist he is, I believe, exemplary in treating all serious critical inquiry with even-handedness and detachment. Typically, he insisted on reading over my typescript to check for errors of fact (after all, I am too young to have been around when many of the events occurred). But on the critical opinions he made no comment, insisting quite rightly that, for those of us who express our views here, the responsibility for error must be ours alone.

Ian Smith
London 2005

Index